GUIDING CHILDREN:

THE GOAL IS HAPPINESS

GEORGE C. BRADLEY
AND
TINA MARSHALL-BRADLEY

Guiding Children is a fascinating story of one couple's real-life child rearing journey focusing on each key child development stage of a person's life. Reading this book will give confidence and encouragement to expecting parents, parents, grandparents, and other responsible adults. Accomplished educators and scholars, George and Tina share their very personal journey and experiences, supported by research-based theories, on how to get parenting right while rearing well-adjusted and productive world citizens.

Henry N. Tisdale, Ph.D.
President Emeritus, Claflin University

This timely book is required reading for anyone interested in effective parenting. It is also mandatory and pertinent reading for young parents who wish to understand the concept and theory of child development. This is a superlative narrative of the Bradley's theory based parenting story. It is an extremely readable book that unites a theory of parenting in an innovative and useful manner. They provide the tools, in this book, gained from their successful rearing of two children, who are engineers with terminal degrees from prestigious universities. This book constitutes an important addition to current literature on parenting and child development. Drs. George and Tina Bradley write from a comprehensive center and more than 40 years engaged education, research, effective parenting.

W. C. Howard, Ph. D.
CEO, Annie L. Howard & Georgia D. Carter Foundation, Inc.

Dedication

This book is dedicated to those who taught us what it means to parent. Edward Bradley, Sudie Bradley Moses, Robert Edward Marshall, Sr. and Jannie Kennedy Marshall

CONTENTS

INTRODUCTION

"Peace is the beauty of life.
It is sunshine. It is the smile of a child, the love of a mother,
the joy of a father, the togetherness of a family.
It is the advancement of man,
the victory of a just cause, the triumph of truth."

-Menachem Begin

The family is a critical unit of society and also a very powerful unit because of the pivotal role it plays. Since the dawn of humanity, our society has always reflected the working dynamics of the family. When families thrive, society thrives, and when the micro-unit we call family fails, society bears the full brunt of that failure. In the last few decades, society has witnessed a gradual evolution in the family structure. In their book on the sociology of family, Deborah Chambers and Pablo Garcia (2021) identify family structures that include single-parent families, cohabiting couples, post-divorce and blended families, same-sex unions, living apart but together (LATS), families of choice, friends as family, and queer intimacies.

This change is majorly reflected in our environment. Broken people have emerged from broken homes, contributing to the emergence of a broken society. This is not to say that there are not people getting it right with their families because there are successful families of all kinds. Although a family need not be perfect, it ought to be stable to a certain degree.

The societal forces we refer to are the fabric that holds a family together. It might be considered its essence. The core of that essence are those individuals who are the primary caregivers of children. People who love and support children are the keys to their success, regardless of family structure; whether a single parent, a family with two parents of the same sex, foster parents, grandparents rearing children, adoptive parents, or a male and female rearing their biological child, people who love and support children are the keys to their success.

It is the foundation provided and the values modeled and promoted that eventually create a structurally sound unit capable of rearing people who are grounded in most facets of life. Indeed, our misplaced priorities, unrealistic expectations, and general unpreparedness for our roles as caregivers for children have all played significant roles in shaping society.

However, even with the challenges faced by families, we have the power to work better and support each other in our roles as caretakers of children. This power does not need any endorsement from a bill passed by the government or any external force. All that is required is the right decision to accept the challenge of raising strong and rational adults.

Let the mistakes made by our predecessors and our personal mistakes inform our decision to learn the right lessons and improve. One cannot deny that help is needed to make the right decisions. Time and experience have taught us the importance of sharing our truth, and that is the essence of this book.

We had the pleasure of rearing two very accomplished adult children. Both have doctorates in engineering and attended college on scholarships. They both travel and are truly world citizens. Our son was a standout high school and college athlete, while our daughter speaks four languages beyond English (Portuguese, Japanese, Spanish, and French). Furthermore, she is raising her children to be multilingual.

It is not just that the children have successfully obtained degrees and have good careers, but they are kind and compassionate beyond these formal accomplishments. All of their lives, we have always received compliments from teachers, friends, and even strangers on how well-rounded they are.

When the children were younger, we were usually at odds with friends, family, and professional colleagues because of some of the decisions we made. Notably, we were very intentional in our choices while raising our children. And the outcomes tell the story. As parents, the only thing they are doing with their respective partners that we did with them is being intentional about how they raise their children. This book is intended to inspire others to be intentional about how they raise their children.

Along the line, you may feel lost, confused and anxious about your role as a parent or caregiver in supporting the development of your children. Never give up; these feelings, although helpful in ensuring that your focus is on the child's best interest, must give way to a more purposeful and strategic way of thinking. The tools we provide in this book in the form of sharing our experiences and information will help you get started on that path. It does not matter if you are just starting on your journey as a parent or if your children are adults with their own children. We focus on each key developmental stage of a person's life.

Each chapter provides you with a PREMISE for what to expect, in general, regarding your child's development. It prepares you for some of the challenges you might encounter and provides you with possible ways to think about supporting children and young people. Our own personal PERSPECTIVES are some of our child-rearing stories and give insights into some of those issues based on our experience.

Finally, in this journey, you are given practical and actionable tips to consider in the form of PROMISES. These are not promises that we are making regarding the way that your child will turn out. These are the promises that every life has to offer when given the right amount of love and attention. We think of this book as a very intimate journal that chronicles our parenting journey, except that we wrote it with you in mind.

There are general expectations for what a child should or should not be doing at a certain stage. We must remember that every child is unique. Even identical twins have their individual milestones. We hope you learn to embrace those differences and cherish every moment. That is not to say your principles should change to adapt to these differences. It is your approach to implementing those principles that may change. Your task is to lay a foundation that prepares children to live their very best lives. Since no one can account for the future, we must prepare ourselves so we can achieve the best possible outcomes based on what we have access to today.

George and Tina

THE SAN FRANCISCO GREAT GRAPE RACE

Preamble

When I was a young adult, I could have sworn that my brother, Tony, told me a story that someone told him. The story was about the San Francisco Great Grape Race. I remember the key components of the story and recounted them like a mantra throughout my life. I thought that this story was so appropriate for parenting. The story formed the foundation for how I would think about parenting as we reared our children. When we started writing this book, I thought a lot about this story, and it formed a central part of my thinking as a parent.

I wanted the story to be accurate, and I also wanted to give credit to the original author. I did an Internet search trying to find the story. I found nothing resembling what I was told. When I asked Tony about the story, he doesn't remember ever telling me this story. I think that it is such an awesome story, but it appears as if I may have just made it up. However, if anyone knows this or a similar story, I hope they will reach out to us.

The Story

The residents of one San Francisco neighborhood have an annual ritual of racing grapes down the steep three-block hill that runs through their community. For bragging rights, the person whose grape successfully makes it to the bottom wins. For many years, this race has taken place annually.

Individuals are given a single grape at a time, and the goal is to be the first to get the grape to the bottom of the hill.

Racers can use anything in the environment to assist. However, they can never pick the grape up off the ground. If for some reason the grape is lost or destroyed, the racer must return to the top of the hill, get another grape, and start the process over.

A visitor to this community became intrigued with the behavior of the racers. She was particularly interested in the strategies that different racers used. Over the years, she would return to the neighborhood to witness the San Francisco Great Grape Race. She took copious notes about the race and the behavior of the racers. After several years she started to see certain patterns and could predict with a fair amount of accuracy which racer would win based on the strategy employed for racing their grape.

The researcher put all racers into three categories based on their strategies. The categories were laissez faire, pusher, and guide. The primary strategy the laissez-faire racer used was to select a good spot at the start of the race, place their grape on the ground, and push it. The strategy used by the pusher was to put the grape on the ground and find some type of object to propel the grape to move. The strategy of the guide was a blend of the first two strategies.

It will interest you that most of the San Francisco Great Grape Race winners were the guides. If your question is "why do the guides always win?" then here is the answer.

At the start of the race, laissez-faire racers look around and identify the best place at the top of the hill to start their grape. They look for an area that is not crowded but is located where the grape will get the maximum velocity. Laissez-faire racers place their grapes carefully and then give them a good thrust. The grape travels down the hill on its own accord. If it stops, the racer gives it another push. However, if the grape goes off track and rolls into the gutter or under the feet of other racers, the laissez-faire racer simply considers it as fate and returns to the top of the hill to start over with another grape or even gives up on the race.

The pusher uses objects in the environment to propel their grapes. They set their grape down and push and prod the grape, trying to get it to roll faster than the other grapes in the race. The problem with the strategy of the pusher is that most times, in their exuberance to make the grape roll faster or stay on track, they use too much force and end up smashing the grape with the object they are using to propel the grape. Having destroyed their grape, they return to the top of the hill for another grape and start the process over or simply give up.

The strategy used by guides is to select the right place to start their race. They also select an object from the environment. They give their grape a push. Instead of focusing only on speed, they watch the grape's direction. If the grape appears to be headed for the gutter or under the feet of other racers, the guide uses the stick, board or other objects to change the direction that the grape is going. If the grape is rolling in the right direction, it does not matter if it wobbles or slows; it is allowed to progress without interference from the guide. The guide repeats this process until the grape reaches the bottom of the hill. The grapes that are raced by guides generally do not roll faster, nor are they directed with the most accuracy. It is a combination of just the right amount of pushing and nudging coupled with support and direction that typically makes for Great Grape Race winners.

In our parenting, we consider ourselves guides. Tina, started out as a pusher. She had predetermined ideas about what she wanted the children to do and be and did everything in her power to push that agenda. George was a more laissez faire parent. He thought we should allow the children to grow and develop naturally to be what they were going to become. His focus was on keeping them safe and healthy.

It wasn't until the results of the pushing strategy were not having the desired outcome, especially with our first born, that as a mother I stepped back. To be honest, I gave up and decided if I let their father take the lead and they were not successful, I could blame him.

Ultimately we grew to become guides. We found our parenting stride. As we grew as a family, we figured out based on our personalities Tina was better suited as primary parent when the children were young and George was the better guide as the children got older. We learned from each other and modified our styles in support of the two people that we were raising. We hope that as you read this book you will see the advantages of being guides.

MIDNIGHT'S CHILDREN: AGES 0-2

"The wonder of life begins in the womb of a woman."

-Lailah Gifty Akita

PREMISES

We rarely stop thinking about the developmental milestones that humans go through from the time of conception until birth. But this early developmental experience lays the foundation for development in the years after birth.

Since prenatal developmental experiences are entirely different from those that an infant goes through once they are born, we'll treat the prenatal developmental markers independently before proceeding with the infancy developmental milestones. The human gestation period that starts with fertilization and concludes with birth lasts about 266-280 days (38-40) weeks. We would not be wrong to assume that development in the prenatal stage is majorly physiological since it involves the formation of all the human body parts.

Physical development in the first two years of birth is extremely rapid. Physical development takes an 'upper to lower' (cephalocaudal development), and an 'inner to outer pattern' (proximodistal development), which means the upper parts of the body develop first before the lower parts and the inner parts of the body develop before the extremities, a factor that greatly defines the infant's motor skills.

By the first month, an infant can lift their head while prostrate and turn their head to the side of an object touching their cheek. At two months, the infant can make finer movements with their legs and arms, hold their head, and push up when lying on the tummy. However, by the fourth month, infants do not need support to hold their heads and can easily bring their hands to their mouth. They have greater control of the extremities and can tightly hold and shake a toy and push down their legs with their feet on the ground. Your four-month-old infant can also roll over when lying on the tummy to lie on their back.

In the sixth month, infants easily roll over in any direction and sit without support. They can rock forward and backward on their knees and palms and bounce on their feet when standing. Between nine and 12 months, infants can crawl with ease, sit up without support, pull to stand and stay standing while holding on, and even cruise (walk while holding on to something). The infant may also stand alone for a while and take a few steps without holding on.

In the 18th month, infants can walk alone, climb stairs, run, pull toys along, remove their clothes, and even drink from a cup and use a spoon to eat by themselves. By the time they complete two years, infants can climb onto chairs, climb up and down the stairs while holding on, run, kick, and throw balls.

At birth, infants have the full visual ability for objects and colors but cannot see further than 15 inches. By the second month, they can notice faces and follow people and objects around with their eyes. At four months of age, infants can respond to affection with a smile, reach out for objects with a single hand, and simultaneously control hand and eye movement by reaching out for what they are looking at. They can turn from one side to the other when a person or object they are following with their eyes does the same, and recognize familiar faces from a distance.

By the time they are six months old, infants are more object-oriented and less self-occupied and will visually show attention to things around them; they will try to reach out to objects that are out of reach but interest them. They can easily put items in their mouth and move objects from one hand to the other.

At nine months, your infant can visually follow the path of a falling object and search for objects that you have hidden from them. By the time they are one year old, infants will show great advancement in cognitive development by exploring the nature of objects through banging, shaking, or dismantling. These actions are often repeated for their consequences. For example, they'll shake a toy to repeat the rattling sound. They can also coordinate their sensory, perceptual, and motor skills, relate names with objects or pictures, imitate gestures, and follow simple instructions like "take the toy."

By their second birthday, infants can easily find hidden stuff, scribble, and name pictures in a book. They can sort objects by shape and color and even build small object towers. They tend to show preference in using one of their hands and complete rhymes or sentences they are familiar with. By now, the infant can also execute two-task instructions like "pick the toy and put it on the table." As a parent, you need to focus on socioemotional development, which examines emotions, temperament, and personality development at various human life stages.

In the first two months after birth, infants are trying to adapt to the new world and will constantly try to calm themselves by sucking their hands when distressed. They make attempts to look at their caregiver even though most of their interaction with the mother is through scent and touch. Then in the fourth month, an infant will spontaneously smile at people and will smile when people play with them or cry when they stop. At this age, infants may also imitate facial expressions like smiles or frowns. By the sixth month, the infant recognizes familiar faces, expresses pleasure when familiar people play with them, and begins to react to other people's emotions.

At one year old, infants may show a preference for particular adults and show fear of strangers and particular situations. For example, they may cry when either of their parents leaves. They also have favorite toys and experiences and may hand you an object, such as a cup, to communicate their desire for a drink or repeat actions and sounds to draw your attention. They will enjoy participating in more complex games such as "pat a cake."

Upon a closer look at them on their second birthday, infants become a bit more independent and will explore by themselves but with parents close by. They will play pretend games like feeding a doll or driving a car to imitate their parents. They want others to join them in play and may give you a play toy so you can join their game. They'll readily include other infants and children in their games and show excitement at their presence. Infants at this age might also throw a tantrum to show displeasure or imitate another infant and may do what they are told not to do to show defiance. These behaviors are evident as a parent or caregiver if you pay attention to them.

Emotions are the first language used by newborns to communicate with their caregivers and show distress, satisfaction, or call for attention, primarily through crying. The response of the mother to the newborn's communication sets the pace for attachment. Between the second and fourth months after birth, infants communicate by making noises that we call cooing, which is a gurgling sound made at the back of the throat. They also respond to sound by turning their head toward the source.

The question of whether children are born with a moral sense is debatable to date. In developmental psychology, reference to the contributions of Piaget and Kohlberg in the study of moral development barely focused on the moral development of infants. Later, developmental psychologists and evolutionary biologists have supported the notion that infants are born with unlearned moral universals and that young infants have rudimentary moral capacities.

You can agree with me that in the first two years of life, infants show a sense of morality in a variety of ways that also characterize adults:

- They can determine whether a third-party interaction is positive or negative in the first months of life.

- They have concern for others who are in pain or sorrow and make an effort to console them.

- They give help to people even when it costs them, which indicates that helping is innate and intrinsically fulfilling.

- They show attraction to people who do good and aversion to those who do what is considered harmful and even try to reward the good and punish the bad.

Developmental psychologists suggest that these markers of moral capacity and development are not entirely learned from cultural and linguistic contexts but have an innate nature, forming the basis for moral cognition in later life. Nevertheless, this assertion is debatable.

By the fourth to sixth month, infants can babble by producing a string of vocalizations ("eh," "ah") and attempt some consonants ("m ... b ..."). They can imitate sounds made by animals or people, and love repeating sounds made by their parents. Infants at this age will make varied crying sounds to show distress, fatigue, or pain. The infant also makes different sounds to communicate joy and satisfaction. They also show recognition of their name when called.

By the time they are nine months to one year old, infants make more precise sounds. It's at this stage you'll hear them say "dada" or "mama," repeat sounds of words you say, and respond to verbal instructions. They can point at things with their fingers, shake their head to say they do not want to eat when you feed them, or wave to say bye.

Between the 18th month and two years of age, infants move from saying several single words to making four-word sentences, coordinate words with gestures like shaking their head while they say "no," and choose from objects by pointing to show you their preference. They can also point to images of things you mention and repeat words heard in a conversation.

Like it or not, a woman's womb is a child's first environment while nature runs its course. The mother's health and well-being is essential, which suggests why rapt attention should be given to the mother's physical and emotional state. Other family members ought to contribute to providing the best environment possible for pregnant women. During pregnancy, women carry the baby, and some members of the family, particularly men, may feel inadequate or constantly stressed out. One challenge that women have is making healthy choices while they are pregnant.

It is a fact that pregnancy causes changes in a woman's body, and impacts their personalities because of fluctuating hormone levels. Expecting mothers may experience mood swings, a sharp decline or (in some cases) an increase in sexual libido, as well as physical discomfort. Some women manage these changes with little difficulty, while other women struggle.

The last stage is more of the cute stuff. You can watch your child smile toothlessly, listen to their joyous laugh, and watch how fascinated they can become with something as simple as a feather. There are so many things to think about. New families must consider where the baby sleeps, who takes care of the baby when some adults in the house are at work, and what will the baby eat in their first months of life. There are many decisions that families must make, including paper or cloth diapers, breast or bottle feeding, and home care or daycare.

From when your child is born right up to when they are two years old, they undergo rapid physical and emotional changes. During this stage of a baby's development, one can expect the following:

At birth, most babies weigh between five and a half pounds to ten pounds. Babies' weight almost doubles within the first six months. By the time they are two years old, they will weigh twenty-five to thirty pounds. In the first few weeks, your baby will not be able to control their movement, so many of the movements you see are involuntary and reflexive. As they grow older, they gain more control. By one month, they can lift their chin when you lie them on their belly. With each month, movement becomes more coordinated.

Note that by the time they are two years old, they can typically walk, run, jump, and perform some complex tasks on their own. Families need to remember that every child develops differently, and the milestones that are identified are generalized. If the child is being diagnosed by a health professional and there is nothing organically wrong with the child, families should simply enjoy their child's physical development.

As you pay attention to them, infants will tend to communicate their feelings in sophisticated ways. Most people recognize crying as a way infants communicate their need for attention. Babies may have a specific type of cry for a specific need. There is the high-pitched wail that indicates hunger. Then the cry that borders on whimpering could indicate diaper change. The worst would have to be that sad, pitiful, never-ending cry that happens when they are in pain (usually after they go for the scheduled immunization shots). But their emotional scope is more than cries. Some emotions are instinctual and naturally occurring, but for the most part, emotions are learned through human interaction. In the first couple of days, babies usually turn to voices they have often heard while in utero. They will hold eye contact with individuals who are speaking to them.

By the time they are four months old, babies can detect the emotional expressions of others. By six months, they can distinguish people better, and at this stage, they may express their discomfort when strangers carry them.

In the ninth month, they become highly emotional and can go from very happy to very frustrated in a few short minutes. At this age, they experience a range of emotions, including surprise, disgust, joy, and fear. At around 11 months old, they learn to regulate those emotions. When they hit the one-year mark, in general, they develop more complex emotions thanks to their heightened emotional awareness that enables them to recognize their own emotions, and the emotions of others.

At this stage, they are particularly aware of when primary caregivers and others around them experience extreme emotions such as happiness or distress. By the time they are two, they understand emotions well enough to use them manipulatively. They can fake being hurt to get your attention. And they can also recognize when they have hurt others and know to apologize for it.

From birth to age two, babies use their senses and actions to learn and grow. They are born with complex cognitive skills to get them started in life. These skills help them recognize and respond to you and any other caregiver who is consistently present in their life. At birth, their vision is not very good, but as their vision develops, fixed focal length stares allow them to memorize the contours of your face and then objects around them.

Their auditory abilities help them pick up the sound of their mother's voice over other noises and to even recognize the voices of those that they have heard often while they were in utero. By the time they are one week old, they can distinguish the sound of your voice and respond to it. By the time your baby is two, they will begin to develop the ability to create and store mental images. At this point, they watch what happens in their environment and then later imitate it. If you have ever seen a child speaking into a phone even though there is no one at the other end, they are demonstrating this new-found skill. This is a pivotal moment in their learning stage.

PERSPECTIVES

Motherhood - Tina

This is my little story and journey to motherhood. On a very beautiful day, I remember every detail of the room I was in when I called the doctor's office to get the results of my first pregnancy test. When I received the news, it felt like all of the air had been sucked out of that room as I tried to make sense of what I was being told. I was pretty sure when I had the test that it would be positive, but since I was a senior in college and unmarried, it was not what I wanted to hear. I called George to break the news using that same beige rotary dial phone and a calling card. It was the middle of the day, and I remember being terrified that he would not pick up the phone. He did answer and seemed very calm considering the news that I was conveying. He was also a college student, and neither of us were employed. My first thought after telling him was about what my parents would think. I was terrified, worried, and in some ways, embarrassed.

I often compare the feeling I had when I found out I was pregnant with my first child to the day I received a call, like many others, from my daughter on a chilly February morning. I could tell that there was something on her mind that she wanted to tell me, but she kept talking about mundane things. After a few moments, I asked what was on her mind. She said she didn't want to tell me, but I insisted. She told me that because she missed her period at 2:00 p.m. the day before, she went and took a pregnancy test, which was positive. My first reaction was to laugh and ask how she thought that she could predict her cycle to within hours. She said she didn't want to say anything because she wasn't sure and wanted it to be true. I remember feeling incredibly happy to hear that my daughter might be pregnant even though she was still in college. I was relieved, overjoyed, and in all ways delighted.

Not only was I chronologically young while I carried my first child, I was also emotionally young. Within a couple of months of finding out that we would be parents, George and I got married, completed undergraduate degrees and moved from our parents' homes to a very small brick structure in a trailer park. I had not prepared my body for pregnancy, but I did my best to eat things that were good for the baby after discovering I was pregnant. George and I were in college during my first pregnancy. While I researched the possible things that would happen to babies during pregnancy, my father also supported me with reading materials. For instance, I remember reading that the baby could hear voices after the first trimester. When George visited me, he would read children's books and sing to the baby. Although his choice of songs irritated me to no end at the time, and I soon realized that our circumstances were not ideal, I had the benefit of being physically, socially and emotionally supported during my pregnancy. While my social circle was amazing, and I had the good sense to embrace their love, I was also emotionally immature and focused too much attention on what other people were thinking instead of embracing my journey to motherhood.

My euphoria at learning Nia was expecting her first child was undoubtedly influenced in part by the fact that her pregnancy occurred as a result of a socially acceptable situation. She was married, and the baby's father was her husband. Although she was a student, she was in the middle of her doctoral studies and had already completed two degrees. She, too, was able to carry her first child in a physically, socially, and emotionally supportive environment. However, unlike my experience, she appeared to embrace impending motherhood with a sense of enthusiasm that was infectious. I downloaded the app that she used to monitor the baby's growth and read along with her about what was happening with her body. I read the books that she was reading along with her. I marveled at the questions that she asked not only me but other members of the family.

I was impressed with the fact that she embraced opposing advice, but her decisions about her pregnancy and child rearing were her own. I also learned how to treat her as an adult child, and it was a liberating experience.

My Hero - George

My thoughts always go to thoughts of my earliest memory of being parented. I was told that when I was one and a half years old, Ed Bradley visited my mother's aunt. Ed would ultimately marry my mother and take on the responsibility of being my father. I was told that the one thing I really loved was my bottle. Even though I was close to two years old, I was still allowed to keep my bottle. If anyone tried to take it away, I would scream until they left me alone. However, when Ed came into our lives, he told me to give him the bottle. Not only did I give it to him right away, but I was also told that I never picked up another bottle. Even at that young age, it appeared that something about him made me want to please him. This adoration would continue for the rest of his life.

Standing His Ground - Tina

When Curtis was three years old, we enrolled him in a learning center in Daytona Beach, Florida. We thought that giving him structured academic engagement would benefit his cognitive growth and psycho-social development. The learning center focused a lot on engaging the children in practical experiences. There was always one story after another about Curtis. There was a time he took over the lesson and demonstrated what one does in a restaurant. The teacher recounted that while they were explaining the process, Curtis jumped up, grabbed a towel, threw it over his left arm and perfectly demonstrated what happens in a restaurant. As everyone watched in amazement, he played the role of the server giving the students a list of the "day's specials." After taking orders, he served his classmates and brought their bills. The teachers then explained that they even knew how we typically paid when we go out to eat because Curtis gave the students a choice of paying by cash or with a credit card. He did not wait for their responses; he just immediately simulated the swiping of a credit card.

On another day, the children were to learn the full names of their family members so that in an emergency, they would not only know mommy, daddy, or grandma. When the teacher asked his mother's name, Curtis said, "Tina." When they asked his father's name, Curtis said, "Mr. Bradley." Confused, the teacher said, "I know his name is Mr. Bradley, but what is his first name?" Curtis said, "My father is a teacher, and you will call him Mr. Bradley." Needless to say that his teachers found Curtis's engagement and social commentary to be quite amusing.

Supporting Aspirations - Tina

One of Curtis's teachers approached me when I came to pick Curtis up from his preschool class. The teacher indicated that she was concerned about Curtis, and she asked us to work with him at home. They were working with the children on future aspirations. When they asked Curtis what he wanted to be when he grew up, he said he wanted to be a lion. That's funny right? Let's continue.

When they tried to explain to Curtis that he could not be a lion and provided him with more appropriate options, Curtis stood fast and insisted that one day he would be a lion. The teacher asked me if I would help Curtis understand that he cannot be a lion. I specifically told the teacher that we would not do that because we did not know that one day he would not be a lion.

Philosophically, we have always believed that if individuals, particularly young children, say that they want to be or do something, then we should help them understand the steps they should consider taking to accomplish their goal. Then our role is to serve as a resource and motivator as they embark on their journey. We always use the example of thinking about what would have happened if, in 1933, Neil Armstrong told the adults around him that one day he wanted to walk on the moon and they told him that he would not be able to do that and suggested that he work towards a more suitable goal.

I am a Father - George

I remember the day that Curtis was born. I was surprised he was not a very large baby, because prior to delivery he appeared to be, and I was elated he was a boy. One of my earliest memories is that we would put Curtis in our bed when we went to sleep. When he woke up for early morning feedings, I would get his bottle and Tina would feed him in bed. This habit would later cause problems. When he started sleeping through the night, and we wanted him to sleep in his crib, he would cry until we put him in bed with us. One night we were determined not to get him out of his crib. In the middle of the night, I opened the door to our bedroom and almost stepped on him because he was lying in front of our bedroom door. With this lesson learned, we ensured that Nia slept in her crib from the first night she came home from the hospital.

Even as a toddler, Curtis was very aggressive. He played very rough and favored older children over children his age. His aggression made me happy because I believed he would always be able to protect himself. I found that people either loved the fact that he was aggressive or found it to be problematic. Along with being aggressive, he was a very stubborn toddler. Tina worked with him on most of the academic tasks. I remember her reading to him and trying to teach him simple concepts. He would never repeat the information, and we were concerned that he wasn't learning. Then one day we would hear him playing by himself and counting or reciting the alphabet. But he refused to do it on demand. We were often embarrassed when we tried to show friends or family members that Curtis could do something, and he would refuse. Eventually we learned to stop trying to demonstrate to others that our son knew or could do something.

I took a lot of pride in having Curtis hang out with me. This practice made many of the men that I socialized with uncomfortable. I told my friends that my son could go anywhere that I went. Some of the situations were not ideal for a toddler because of things like adult language being used. I felt that it was more important for Curtis to spend time with me even if the situations were not what most people considered appropriate for a child. This early involvement with just the two of us set the foundation for our relationship throughout our lives.

PROMISES

From our experience, we can tell you that the issues that you will encounter as a parent are both beautiful and terrifying. Thinking about the fact that you will now be responsible for another person's life is profound. With the right application of knowledge, you can manage the situation and enjoy a positive outcome.

Families can help a pregnant woman make the most of her pregnancy by ensuring that she eats a healthy and varied diet. Some nutritional supplements claim to help provide quality brain food for babies, but nothing beats real and fresh food. Expectant mothers should try to eat the best quality food possible. A 2018 study by the Burke Foundation supports the idea that exercising during pregnancy can boost a child's brain's memory and learning center. Exercise also has health benefits for mom.

Family members can support the mother by making similar healthy choices. Alcohol consumption and smoking are two habits that healthcare providers advise mothers to avoid in order to have a healthy pregnancy. Family members ought to stop these activities for the period of the pregnancy. This one act is a show of solidarity and support. If family members do not wish to stop these activities completely, they can refrain from engaging when mom is around. Not only does this have a good impact on the health of the mother and child, but it can also help to strengthen her resolve. Furthermore, families can also support expecting mothers by joining them in making healthy meal choices and engaging in daily exercise routines. If not for anything else, then they should do so for the fact that there is strength in numbers.

There are times that we forget the very important role that fathers play during the gestation process. Since babies can hear after the first trimester, the voice of the father can provide the baby with comfort. Fathers should talk, read, and sing to the baby in utero. Actively supporting the mom while she is caring for the baby is just as important as the healthy steps that the mother is taking. Setting aside unhealthy habits while engaging in healthy habits, if only for the period of the pregnancy, supports the mom as she is caring for the baby while giving the baby the best foundation possible.

Consideration should be given to other members of the family. A balance between the attention given to older siblings and other members of the household can ease stress. You should not assume that others know what you are feeling. Setting aside time to discuss daily activities and feelings is worthwhile. If increasing the amount of vegetables that the family eats causes unhappiness among older siblings, that may not be a battle that the family wants to fight. A few intentional changes that are made and kept are more important than a lot of drastic changes that cause people in the family to be unhappy or resentful.

Before the baby is born, so many resources are available to families to support the child and family. Hospitals and clinics offer courses for parents, grandparents, siblings, and in some cases, even pets. Even if this is not the first child to be born in the family, these learning opportunities are great activities to form bonds. Classes are a way to actively involve other children and other members of the family in activities surrounding the birth of the child. And you may also learn something.

It is essential that you consider the environment in which the baby will live as a parent or caregiver. Regardless of your budget, you can create a stimulating environment for the new baby. The environment should include bright colors and be visually stimulating without being too busy. You do not have to invest in expensive items to hang on the wall or from the baby's bassinet or crib. Many libraries have various resources that can be checked out and used. Along with being visually stimulating, the baby's environment should include a variety of sounds. There should be opportunities for the baby to hear different sounds, including various kinds of music and sounds from nature.

Notwithstanding that your baby spends most time alone, the sights and sounds of family members brings comfort to the baby. When holding the baby, make sure you hold them as close to your face as possible. Initially, babies do not see well at a distance. Babies respond to human faces. While feeding them or rocking them, be in the moment and pay attention to them. This is not the time to engage on your mobile devices. In fact, when reading to a baby, check out books with portraits of diverse people.

The human voice is one of the best sounds you can provide the new baby. Talking to a baby does more for their social, cognitive, and emotional development than any media. Make sure that you use actual words when communicating with the baby. Although babies may respond positively to your babbling, they are responding to your voice's intonation. When you speak like you would to an adult, the cadence of your voice stimulates the baby and exposes them to words that help them build their vocabulary. If you have ever tried to learn another language, you know the importance of hearing the exact words repeatedly. The same is true for babies, who are learning their very first language.

Because babies do not speak back, we forget that they communicate very well. Hospital personnel have reported newborn babies responding to the sound of the voices of individuals they have heard while in utero. Babies will smile, laugh, and warble at silly faces and singing. They also become sad when individuals are near them but do not actively engage with them. Family members should use various words to increase the baby's vocabulary and use every waking moment to talk to the baby.

After years of living primarily in rural communities, the world population is now more situated in urban environments. We have moved away from lands where we saw food growing and moved to environments where time is important, and we increasingly do things fast. The advent of fast food establishments worldwide has seen an impact on people's health to the point that there is a boom of resources devoted to consuming foods that are in season and grown close to where the food is being consumed.

When a child is born, considering how the child develops physically is based partly on the food they consume. Families living in traditional societies have focused on breastfeeding for newborns because they cannot access formulas. We know more about the long-term health benefits of breastfeeding infants, particularly in the first few months of life. This is an important period not only for physical development because of what is being consumed, but breastfeeding is important for how babies are fed. It is important for babies to look into the eyes of the adults who are feeding them. They need to hear the heartbeat of the person who is feeding them. Breast-feeding also offers the opportunity for adults to revisit their eating habits.

If you opt for formula feeding, you can use the feeding moments to create positive experiences just like you would if you were breastfeeding. Eye contact, skin contact, and smiling at the baby are brain-building activities you can engage in during the first few weeks of their lives. Fathers can also be a part of this experience by handling the feeding duties from time to time, whether the baby is consuming breast milk or formula.

Feeding time is a particularly important time for babies as it is at these times when their cognitive skills can be developed. Family members should hold infants when they are being fed. Early in their lives, adults should hold the baby as close to their faces as possible, look into their eyes and talk with or sing to them. From this activity, babies develop a sense of trust and begin to understand that they are safe and protected.

Most babies take to breastfeeding easily, but it is not always an easy process. As a mother, you should not suffer in silence but seek the consultation of a lactation consultant or a supportive family member or friend who can offer practical solutions. The idea is to be patient with yourself if you are the mother. If you are a partner, it is essential to be loving and supportive while the mother is engaged in the process of breastfeeding. If you start your child with positive eating rituals that include paying attention to what they eat and engaging with others while they eat, those habits will last a lifetime. Other things to consider with infants include:

1. **Make mealtime fun:** You can never talk too much to babies. Stimulating conversations, singing, and laughter are all good things to practice during mealtimes. Consider telling the baby stories about family members or narratives about events in your life.

2. **Feed children real food:** Have you ever wondered what babies ate before there was packaged baby food? They ate the same food that the rest of the family ate. Consider blending simple foods for the baby. Start with fruits and vegetables, feeding the baby the same food for a couple of days. Do not add anything to the food. Feed the baby various foods, allowing their palates to adjust to each food. Did you know that introducing babies to solid food is less expensive and has health benefits?

3. **Vary the foods that they eat:** When children begin to eat solid foods, make sure that you introduce them to a variety of foods that are

different in color, texture, temperature, and taste. When children do not eat a particular food, try giving it to them on another day. It may not be that they dislike the food; they just may not be in the mood for a particular food on a particular day. Resist the urge to force a child to eat. Most experts agree that children can go for a couple of days without eating, unless there is something medically wrong (but typically, this is not the case). When they are hungry, they will surely eat.

4. **Portion control:** Present babies with an appropriate amount of food. Allow them to stop eating when they are done, even if more food is left. Take your cue as to how much food to feed the baby from the baby. When they are no longer interested in the food, stop feeding them. Resist the urge to make babies eat all of the food because that is what you prepared.

5. **Mealtime is for eating:** Let the baby focus on eating as much as possible. When the baby is feeding themself, take the opportunity to have a meal with them. Have pleasant conversations with them about the food that they are eating and other pleasantries. It is never too early to start the happy activity of holding interesting conversations over a nice meal. The conversation may be one-sided for a while. But you may be pleasantly surprised with a baby's ability to engage with you in interesting ways.

One of the biggest direct expenses that families incur with the addition of a new baby is childcare. There is a common misperception that in a two-parent household, both parents must work. Families should consider different options while thinking about welcoming home the new addition to the family.

Families have cut expenses so that one parent can take care of the child full-time. There are options for parents selecting working environments, such as one or both parents working online so that someone is always home with the child. Another option is to have one parent work in the evening while the other works during the day. Thus, childcare can be shared by both parents. Still another option is to have one parent work full-time while the other works part-time. Some families invite family members to stay with or near them and to watch the baby while they are at work. Some of these options mean a decrease in family income or an inconvenience, but it also decreases expenses related to childcare and increases the time that the baby is with loved ones.

Suppose it is not possible to plan for the baby to be cared for by a member of the family. In that case, the childcare option selected for the baby must ensure they are safe, clean, well fed and appropriately stimulated. It is natural for children who are in environments with other children to catch more colds and viruses than children who are kept in private care or at home. Families should make sure that the adults who are taking care of the baby change their diapers constantly so as not to cause skin irritations. You want to make sure that babies are being fed a healthy diet. You also want to ensure that the adults taking care of your baby talk and read to them daily.

Another significant expense is the home where the baby will be raised. The baby's primary environment should be safe and free from toxins. When considering the space in the home where the baby will sleep, ensure that the area is clean and clear of clutter. When possible, the area should also be quiet to ensure that when the baby is sleeping, they can get all the rest they need. Sleep is as important to a baby's health as nutrition.

If possible, the baby should never sleep in the same bed as adults or other children. Infants should always have their own sleep spaces. There is nothing magic about a crib or a bassinet. For instance, the government of Finland provides every pregnant woman who gets neonatal services with a baby box. Inside the box are things that the baby will need in the first months of life. Items include bedding, clothing, teething toys, a picture book, cloth diapers, and other useful items for the baby and parents. But as important as the contents in the box, the empty box itself is designed for the baby to sleep in.

In the 1930s, Finland's infant mortality rate was 65 infant deaths per 1,000 births. Recently the infant mortality rate dropped to less than two infant deaths per 1,000 births. This is not all because of the box; the country encourages and supports certain behaviors from the mother and family. Parents should resist the urge to spend large amounts of money on baby furniture.

Babies grow extremely fast, and thus there is no need for a lot of clothes. Purchase only what is necessary for the baby. We have seen new parents spend a lot of money on clothes for the little one because baby clothes are very cute. A large wardrobe for a baby is ego-boosting for parents but does nothing for the health or happiness of the baby. Clothes for the baby should protect them from the elements and keep them comfortable.

In a busy society, we forget about providing the baby with as much fresh air as possible. Families should get in the habit of taking the baby outside for walks or to play in the yard every day. Activities outside expose the baby to the sounds of nature and fresh air. Even short periods of exposure to the elements, such as snow and rain, stimulate the baby's senses.

In the first few weeks that a baby enters a household, family members are smitten with the new addition to the family. In the following weeks, families may start wondering what they are doing wrong as the baby's sleeping habits contradict the rest of the family. There are no quick fixes for babies sleeping through the night. Each person has their own circadian rhythm. However, babies respond to environmental elements, such as noise and light. Families can ensure that babies get enough sleep by:

1. **Setting up a bedtime routine:** Start by setting a specific time for bedtime and sticking with it. Other bedtime routines may include a warm bath or wipe down with a warm cloth. A body massage may include stretching the baby's limbs and rubbing their backs and stomachs in slow rhythmic motions. Family members may also read or tell stories, sing songs, and exchange hugs and kisses. What is done is not as important as that it is consistent.

2. Let the child cry a little: This is difficult for many because it goes against every parenting instinct. Picking a child up as soon as they cry may make it difficult for the baby to learn how to comfort themselves. Self-soothing is a skill that is necessary for sleeping without aid. Ensure the baby is well fed, has changed their diapers, and the room temperature is comfortable.

3. Naps as sleep routine. Like an evening sleep routine, babies should have routines for naps during the day. Ensure that the baby is not hungry, thirsty, or wet. Employ some of the same bedtime routines that you do during the evening. Place the baby in a quiet, comfortable environment with a limited amount of light. Ensure that caregivers comply with this routine.

No one has a classic meltdown quite like the dramatic two-year-old. There is a reason this phase in the child's life is referred to as the terrible twos. Throwing these fits in public places can be a horrifying and embarrassing experience for parents and caregivers. In the middle of the tantrum, adults typically react to the child's behavior as opposed to the reason behind the behavior. There are times that you may understand that the child is tired, hungry, or uncomfortable. Then there are times when there is no logical reason for the tantrum. I know it can be frustrating, but relax. Regardless of the reason, these are some guidelines to consider:

1. **Never lose your cool:**Yes, your nerve ends are probably frayed from all the whining and protests making you want to lash out in return. However, doing this might be interpreted by your toddler as a reward for the stunt they just pulled. Thus, you would increase the possibility of them repeating this behavior. Stay calm and process your next line of action.

2. **Help them understand their feelings:** Children as young as one can start to use breathing techniques to manage their emotions. Ask the child to help you blow up a balloon. Take a deep breath while raising your arms out to your sides and over your head, and encourage your child to do the same. Then blow the air out as if blowing up the balloon making a rasping sound with your lips. You and the child should repeat this three times. Children typically take great delight in making the rasping noise with their mouths. They are also learning a great way of calming themselves down.

3. **Ignore their behavior:** It is easier said than done, but the payoff is rewarding. When they are in the middle of their crisis, calmly inform them that

you would be willing to listen to their complaints whenever they are ready and approach you more reasonably. Then exit the room. If you are in public, turn your attention away from the child.

4. **Model good behavior at home and in public**: Adults may not flop on the ground like a fish out of water, but we throw tantrums as well. Children are like an absorbent sponge, especially at this stage. They would emulate what they see you do. When you become angry or frustrated, blow up your balloon. There is magic in simply breathing.

Between sleep deprivation and the endless cycle of chores, among all the other craziness you are juggling, you can expect to lose your mind every other day. While yelling into a pillow might provide temporary relief, you will need a more sustainable solution in the long run. Save your sanity with these simple tips:

1. **Don't try to be perfect:** Spotless rooms, home-cooked meals, well-behaved children, and completed work projects that garner high praise from your bosses might be your goal. Reality offers a very different narrative. You will find piles of dirty clothes in the laundry bag, siblings squabbling about something trivial, dinner from a pizza box, and looming deadlines are more your day-to-day experiences. This doesn't make you less of a good parent. Besides, perfection is an unrealistic goal; you are better off focusing on what really matters, like ensuring your children are healthy, bills are paid on time, and your home being a safe environment.

2. **Get help:** There is that independent streak in all of us that has us pushing ourselves past our human limit. Some days, we get through it. But there will always be those days that have us feeling overwhelmed. Setting aside our super parent tendencies and getting help [even if it is paid help] can give you room to breathe. On days you feel stretched, hire a cleaning crew for home upkeep or maybe a personal chef to help you with a meal or two. This may cost a little, but that little peace of mind it buys you is totally worth it.

3. **Tap out and take some time off:** People say you can never take time off from being a parent. If time off means long, extended periods without your presence in the life of your child, then no, you can't. However, you could take a day to just focus on yourself. If you are in a partnership like marriage or co-parenting, fix a day for your partner to handle all the parenting duties and use the free time to refresh and renew yourself. For parents going it alone, talk to a relative or hire a sitter for the day. If you have a trusted friend who has children, you could suggest dropping your children off for the day and offer to do the same when they need it.

4. **Schedule yourself in:** Between the PTA meetings, play dates, carpooling and home errands, you rarely have time for yourself. Financially, your needs as a parent often take a backseat. At this stage, their needs are your priority, but you can quickly experience burnout if you don't attend to your needs as well. Setting aside 30 minutes a day when you are neither working nor parenting

can significantly affect your mental health. Waking up an hour or so before the entire house is awake is perfect.

5. **Plan ahead:** You are always better equipped for life when you plan ahead, and in parenting, this still applies. Plan your meals over the weekend to avoid making a frantic dash to the store mid-week in search of ingredients for the makings of dinner. If you know your workload for a specific time might be heavy, make arrangements with your child's caregiver.

The arrival of a child changes the relationship between parents, and those changes are not always good. If not checkmated, the pockets of tension caused by the new arrival could escalate into frightening proportions. When you throw in your work schedule, this can put a significant dent in that relationship. There are tons of books and articles written by experts to address these problems. From our personal experience, the one thing we have always imbibed through-out our relationship is maintaining healthy communication. It doesn't matter what our individual schedules are; com-munication keeps us on the same page and helps us navigate situations that cause friction. Communication is more than just talking to each other. It involves speaking your partner's love language fluently. For some of us, our love language is gifts; for some, it is acts of service. Whatever it is, keeping the doors of communication open is one way to keep the balance in your relationship.

Education starts in the home. When your child is born, they start learning and absorbing information from their environment. A parent is the first teacher for every child, and their ability to excel academically and grow cognitively largely depends on the foundation you lay at home. At this stage, they may fully understand your words, and their attention span is short, so using extended periods to elaborate on certain subjects may not yield specific results.

By age two, your child has discovered his "independence muscle" and may not want to pay attention to you even if they better understand what you are saying. One thing they seem to have boundless energy for is play. Capitalize on their love for play and use games as a teaching/learning opportunity. For younger babies, buy toys that build and engage their motor skills. Giving hugs, maintaining eye contact and using positive affirmations builds them up emotionally and nurtures their confidence, which is essential for learning.

As they grow older, they indulge in role-play games to teach morals, use picture books and visual cards to improve their memory, and use short but funny poems and songs to teach numbers or even new words. The possibilities are endless. You just need to be creative, consistent and patient. While we all want our children to become the next Einstein, resist the urge to enroll them in every child learning activity that pops up on your radar. Swimming lessons, sensory classes, baby gymnastics, and so on have their individual benefits, but signing your children up for all these activities simultaneously can leave your baby stressed. Stress inhibits learning. You need activities that provide a healthy balance of fun, learning, and just letting the children be children.

Every child grows and develops at their own pace. Getting frustrated with how or when they should do certain things will not enable you to be an effective parent to them. If children are healthy, push aside any internal timeline you may have and direct your energies toward understanding them as individuals. Use that knowledge to create the right environment for them to thrive in.

Most importantly, treasure your moments now because time seems to go by quickly. Soon the baby who depended on you completely will be off and exploring the world. And it is that world you want to prepare them for. No matter what happens, please make up your mind to commit to the process and be there for them.

"Having a child is like getting a tattoo … on your face.
You better be committed."

Elizabeth Gilbert

THINGS FALL APART: AGES 3 – 5

"Don't worry that children never listen to you; worry that they are always watching you."

Robert Fulghum

PREMISES

Early childhood in human development usually covers the years between three and five years, depending on the context. Physical development significantly slows down after the first two years of life. Hereditary and nutritional factors are clearly at play in the child's growth in height and weight at this stage. By the end of this stage, children have developed around 95% of their adult brain with refined details in the brain's functioning and slowed the increase in volume.

Concerning their motor skills, children at this age coordinate their body parts better simultaneously. By their third birthday, the muscles and joints are much stronger, and they can climb, run, cycle, and easily support their weight on one leg at a time as they walk up and down stairs. By the time they are four, children tend to stand on one foot, hop, and catch a bouncing ball. Their finer motor skills are also more developed, and they can hold objects between their fingers with greater strength. For example, they will use cutlery when eating fairly well, even though they still struggle with details. By the fifth year, your child can perform fairly complex physical movements without any assistance: skip, somersault, climb, stand for longer on one foot, cut with a table knife, use the toilet without your assistance, and tie their shoelaces with ease.

Children between the ages of three and five years of age are in the preoperational stage of cognitive development. They can now represent their world in words, images, and drawings. These developmental milestones lay the foundation for their mental operations in the next stage. By the time they turn three, they can easily perform several tasks, including turning door handles, effortlessly handle lever and button toys, complete puzzles with a few pieces, turn book pages one at a time, and copy a circle. They can also comprehend small numbers and do pretense-play with people, toys, or animals. Most children at this stage can also open and close jar lids.

Their mental development allows them to mentally represent objects that are not necessarily real or known to them, thus widening their mental world. Mental development also allows them to use drawings to represent realities such as people, houses, and cars, often making the drawings fancy and inventive. For example, you might see your child draw a flying car or a blue sun.

Between four and five years of age, children can name colors, gradually count until they reach 10, print some numbers and letters, copy geometrical shapes, begin to understand time, fairly understand the idea of same and different, and draw a person while gradually increasing the body parts.

Your four to five-year-old will remember parts of stories you've told them, anticipate what will happen in a story, and explain things used in everyday life, such as food and money. Their developed control of motor skills will allow them to do more complex tasks, such as using a pair of scissors. This is also the "stage of a million questions," when your child will ask many questions to understand why reality is different from their imaginative world.

Their exposure to a wider social context leads them to try out new tasks and activities and develop a sense of initiative. But, if their initiative is met by failure and lack of appreciation, children in this stage can develop a sense of guilt. Even though children at this age do not compare what they can do with what their playmates can do but build their sense of worth around what they can do now that they could not do yesterday, parents should be careful not to discourage or compare their child's ability with others.

As part of their developmental initiative, children at the age of three can easily separate from immediate caregivers like the mother and father to explore the reality around them. However, they will still imitate parents, other adults, and friends. three-year-olds will manifest many emotions, including affection and concern for distressed friends. At this age, they can also differentiate what belongs to "me" and what belongs to "her/him" and be able to take turns in games.

At the age of four years, your child will show more creativity in pretend play but will often not differentiate reality from their imagination. The company of other children in play becomes more important than playing alone, and the child readily collaborates with others in play. Four-year-olds will enjoy trying new activities and often speak about what they like or are interested in.

By the time they are five, they can now tell what is real and what is imagined and are aware that men and women, boys, and girls are different. During play, they will want to make their friends happy and be like their friends. Even though they follow play rules, they can sometimes switch from cooperating in play to bossing their playmates. Play is often characterized by ordinary tasks like dancing, singing, or acting.

At this age, you'll need to keep an eye on your child as he/she may have a sense of independence and walk away from your supervision. When it comes to language and communication, your three to five-year-old will show a lot of progress in using words and writing, and in their ability to comprehend what is said to them.

An essential developmental marker at this age is something called private speech. While most parents may wonder why their child is talking to themselves, developmental psychologists explain this as an important developmental experience: children solve their play tasks and regulate their emotions and behavior by talking to themselves. Private speech is also an important indicator of thought development.

Language and communication development markers by the age of three include the child's ability to follow instructions with up to three steps, remembering the names of familiar objects or friends, and describing themselves with their name, age, and sex. They can use pronouns to express themselves and others and say familiar words in their plural form. By this time, children can make themselves understood by strangers and sustain a conversation using up to three sentences at a time.

At the age of four, children tend to show a greater understanding of grammar rules. For example, they will correctly use gender pronouns. Their advanced language skills will also be seen in their capacity to memorize and recite songs or poems or retell stories that were narrated to them. By age five, kids in the early childhood stage can speak clearly and correctly use tenses.

Children in the early childhood stage understand better moral rules and the idea of rightness and wrongness. Furthermore, in this stage, children see moral rules as fixed and absolute, and follow them to avoid punishment. Even in their relations with others, wrong is punished, and good is rewarded. Moral rules are made by those with authority, like parents, and they have the right to punish or reward those who follow or don't follow them.

So, if you should ask your child if it is right to steal another kid's candy, they will say that it's not right because "it is bad to steal." This information is probably based on something that they heard a grown-up or older child say. Or they will say that "you will get in trouble." Even if the child were to justify stealing the candy, their moral justification would still be based on rules and punishment.

PERSPECTIVES

Finding One's Voice – Tina

When Curtis was two years old, we moved to Daytona Beach, Florida. In the process of meeting people, we were introduced to a professional couple in the community. When they came to visit, they had two small children. Their daughter was the exact same age as Curtis. When she came into the house, she introduced herself, stating her first and last name in a complete sentence. At that time, Curtis very rarely spoke in complete sentences and used mostly single words. Some of these utterances could only be described as sounds that we recognized as expressing his desire for something to drink or describing a game he played in the bathtub. However, I was mortified that Curtis's language was so far behind his new little friend's.

I was teaching in the local public schools. At the next available opportunity, I went to the school's speech pathologists and asked what could be done about Curtis's language. The very wise speech pathologist told me to remember that teachers' children are not supposed to be developmentally more advanced than other people's children. He told me that it is also important to remember that children develop at their own pace. He did agree to give Curtis a language screening. Having ignored the speech pathologist's first two statements, I jumped at the opportunity to determine what was "wrong" with Curtis.

The results of Curtis's screening were that he had an eighteen-month speech delay. This information did not seem to make much sense to me. He was speaking entire words and telling us what he wanted or how he was feeling or what he was thinking. He did not use a lot of words, and he did not always speak in full sentences, but he talked. In any case, the speech pathologists encouraged us to continue to read to Curtis, talk to him often, and as often as possible give him our undivided attention when he spoke. The speech pathologist also told us that because there was a delay of over three months, a full screening had to be done by the district.

We had no problem with this requirement, and we prepared Curtis to have a full screening. This included a psychological screening, a more in-depth speech and hearing screening, as well as a review of our home life by a social worker. When the case worker came to share the information with us, she congratulated us because Curtis qualified to be enrolled in the varying exceptionalities resource preschool class in the district. At two years old, he would be able to attend this program that consisted of a class with only four students.

I asked the case worker to explain the tests that were done with Curtis. She said that Curtis had shown diminished psycho-social development. When I asked her to describe the test, the case worker indicated that it was a test that had been created by the district. I asked the case worker to give me some examples of the questions or activities Curtis was asked to do. The case worker happily noted that we had many books in the home and that Curtis had a substantial library, but he was not able to identify several Disney characters. I pointed out that if she took a closer look at Curtis's library, it did not contain one book that featured a Disney character, and in fact, we purposely did not read books with commercial characters. She then said Curtis could not perform another basic task. When asked what time he watches his favorite television show, Curtis could not tell the evaluator. I then explained that Curtis rarely watched television.

It was then that I stopped the review and asked for the parent consent forms where I acknowledged that I understood the evaluation but did not want Curtis to attend the preschool class. We found out later that the preschool special class would have included three students who were at the severe end of the autism spectrum and did not speak at all. We always wondered how being in a class with children who did not talk would benefit our child who needed to increase his language skills.

Learning to Swim - George

When we decided it was time to purchase our first home, we called both sets of parents and received the same advice. We were told that we should buy as much house as we could afford. So we purchased a cute little house in Port Orange, Florida, with a little artificial lake in the backyard. We had not considered that this home had a body of water in the backyard, and we had two young children.

Curtis was three years old, and Nia was one when we purchased our first home.

My worst fear was that one of the children would get out of the house and make their way down to the lake and drown. As a result, I insisted that they take swimming lessons. They learned to swim at a young age. We didn't enroll them in swim lessons because we thought they might compete one day; I thought it was an important skill for them to have.

I'm His Mother – Tina

George spent a lot of time with Curtis when he was a toddler. At times he would take Curtis clothes shopping. I never asked, but he must have let Curtis pick out his own clothes. They were usually things that I would never buy. There didn't seem to be any rhyme or reason to the clothing. Some were pricey, and some were cheap. Rarely did things match. And then, George would allow Curtis to select what he wanted to wear.

Although I was typically mortified with the outcome, I kept my thoughts to myself because you could not miss the pure joy on that child's face when his father dressed him. One of my girlfriends said, "That is fine, but people will ask, 'who is that child's mother?'" And I said, "I will tell them, 'I am his mother. But his father dressed him.'"

Fools and Children - Tina

It has been said that God takes care of fools and children. While rearing Curtis and Nia, God had to take care of us on both fronts. We knew that we needed support with the children and always sought the support of family and friends. There were individuals who became family because they were supporting us with the children.

Particularly when we were in graduate school, we sought out undergraduate students who were away from home and needed an opportunity to get away from campus life. We befriended them, invited them to family dinners, and allowed them to study or cook meals in our apartment. They also became Curtis and Nia's caretakers. Since we were all in school, our schedules were hectic and sometimes subject to change. We would tell the children that someone was transporting them or staying with them. When plans changed, we had to communicate with the children in one way or another that the person who came to get them was someone they could trust.

This was before mobile phones were popular. We developed a system of safe words that we used. We would establish the word, and if there was a change in plans or someone came to the door and they were home by themselves, they were not to go with the person or open the door unless the person used the password. After we used the password outside of the family, we would change it for the next time.

During one of the lessons on using the password and being safe, George asked the children what the password was, and they told him. A couple of days later, the children were home alone, and George knocked on the door. The children followed protocol and asked for the password. George told them that he had forgotten the password. He told Curtis to go get a chair and look through the peephole in the door. When Curtis saw it was his father, he opened the door. George chastised him and told him that no matter what anyone said and even if he looked and saw that it was someone that he knew, they were never to open the door unless the person knew the password.

Months went by, and we came home from the library. When we knocked on the door, the children asked for the password. We gave them the last password we remembered. Curtis told us that it was not the correct password because we changed it after it had been used. As hard as we tried, neither of us could remember the new password. George told Curtis to just look through the peephole in the door, so he could see it was us. Curtis got a chair, looked through the peephole and said, "Hi, Mom and Dad." George then asked him to open the door. Curtis refused. No matter what George said, the children would not open the door. Luckily, we lived on the first floor, and George could break the lock and climb through the window. The children were sitting on the couch watching television. George crawled between them and had to open the door for me because they still would not open the door because we had not given the correct password. There was no way we could be mad.

PROMISES

During this stage, little ones are ready to spread their wings, and you are more comfortable with their independence. There is still the push and pull of how much independence you will allow them. You love the fact that they want to fix their own breakfast, but you don't look forward to cleaning half a gallon of milk off of the floor. These years provide lovely opportunities to spend a couple of extra minutes cleaning up what your children have "cleaned" up on their way to becoming self-sustaining human beings.

Let children be children. Before you know it, they will be independent individuals. At the end of this stage, your child may be starting school. You have to constantly remind yourself that their early learning starts at home and that home is the only constant in the equation. You are not only their first teachers but will also be the consistent presence as they move through life. So, do everything you can to make each waking moment a fun learning opportunity.

The beauty of this age is that learning does not necessarily have to involve books, a board, or a chair. Right in the middle of washing dishes, a learning session can take place. All that is required is fun, a little bit of creativity, and then a lot of consistency on your part. You probably will not notice a difference right away. Just trust the process and be diligent. To help you get started, here are a few tips we thought to share with you.

Confidence is the greatest gift you can give your child. The ability to hold their heads high and stand their ground without being disconnected from reality is truly precious. And just like emotional attributes like empathy, kindness, and the likes, you can teach your children to be confident. Teaching a child to be confident is not like teaching the alphabet. You cannot recite until you gain mastery over it. Building a child's confidence requires consistency and diligence.

True confidence stems from one's sense of self-awareness and ability to embrace failure as a natural part of the growth process. People with high self-worth have a healthy, positive self-image of themselves. Call attention to small wins in your child's life. If they are playing with a puzzle and put two pieces together, congratulate them. Make sure that you celebrate the work and not just the accomplishments. Your children will learn that there is just as much triumph in the work as there is in the outcome of a task.

Giving a child that kind of mentality would lead to an adult with an overinflated ego. Beyond the fact that nobody likes a person with an ego that big, it causes such a person to make reckless decisions because they become deluded about their invincibility. You want to raise a child who is grounded and connected to the reality of what is going on around them. They understand their strengths and flaws but are not overtly overwhelmed by the negatives.

You, as a parent, ought to accept them for who they are; this is very important to their development. Help them develop comfort and confidence in conversing with people of various ages and backgrounds. This will give them a connection to their place in society.

Use positive affirmations. Like water is to a garden, positive affirmations strengthen your child's emotional health. Make sure that your positive affirmations are sincere. Catch your child doing something positive and call it to their attention in a very specific language. Instead of simply saying "good job" when they have cleaned up their room, use specific language such as, "I like the way that you picked up all of the toys off the floor and put them away." Doing this repeatedly provides your child with specific cues on what they did that you would like them to repeat.

Don't try to do everything by yourself. While it might be difficult to watch your three or five-year-old struggle to tie their shoes, leaving them to successfully complete this task will boost their confidence. Even if they are not successful, praising them for trying will go a long way in improving their confidence. When they are successful, reminding them of what they had to do on their journey to success will help them build the capacity to continue to struggle as they learn new things. Remember to apply positive affirmations and then continue to give them more age-appropriate tasks to carry out. Above all, resist the urge to take over, no matter how messy things get. Offer guidance when you can but allow them to complete the task.

Let your child make their own decisions. Giving your children choices at this stage may be scary for parents who believe parenting is about maintaining control. Letting your children make decisions boosts their confidence. Let your three to five-year-old pick out their own clothes. Instead of selecting a bedtime story, always allow your child to select their own book. If you go to a restaurant, allow them to order from the menu. The more opportunities you give them, the more confident they become. And as they grow older, this activity will assist them in making critical decisions.

Resist the urge to set perfection as the standard. In this stage, it is important that they try, fail, and try again in a safe and supportive environment. You have to constantly remind them that the only person they should be in competition with is who they were yesterday. As they begin to learn different things, celebrate their triumphs and encourage them as they continue to learn.

They can be responsible. A great way to instill responsibility is to assign your young child household chores. Start with what is closest to them. When they play with their toys, have them pick them up. Remember to make it a game. They can sing the clean-up song while they are putting their things away. You can even get a stepstool and place it in front of the sink and have your child rinse their dishes after they have finished eating. Children at this age love to help; please allow them. Look at a task such as making a sandwich and allow them to help by gathering the ingredients or placing the ingredients on the bread. As always, use this as a time for bonding.

Be a model. One of the best ways to teach your children responsibility is to be a good role model. If you come home from work and take off your shoes and leave them where they fall instead of putting them away, your children will assume that this is what they are supposed to do. Children emulate actions more than they heed to words. If you want your child to exhibit responsible behaviors, model those behaviors for them.

At any age, learning should be fun, but this is especially true for children in this stage. Given the problem with their short attention span and inability to focus, it is your job to ensure that children remain excited about learning even if they do it every minute of the day. Several teaching methods are effective in simplifying the learning process for children while keeping things exciting at the same time. The challenge is finding what works best for your child, and that is up to you.

Be excited about learning. Children are very perceptive. They know when you are not being authentic. Your sincere interest will inspire your child to want to embrace the task you are engaging in. So, regardless of the topic you are learning together, as they say in the workspace, you have to put your back into it. Sing, dance, wave your hands, and do what you need to do to ensure that learning time is fun.

This does not mean that learning will not be filled with frustration, tears, and disappointment. Resist the urge to shelter your child from these feelings. In fact, lean into them and have your child lean into the feelings; you are not just their parent, you are also their friend. There is nothing more frustrating than watching a toddler put together a puzzle. It is so hard not to help them put their part together. Your heart is broken by their tears and their expressions of frustration. This starts the practice of allowing your child to fall and to figure out how to get back up. This will help them throughout their life.

Go outside. Outside experiences are amazing for physical and mental development. The sunshine or nipping cold on the flesh is something children should experience often. Some of the most memorable learning experiences happen in the natural environment. From watching a butterfly, you are given an opportunity to teach your child about changes in life. Playing around in the garden with the flowers can help them understand more about colors and how intriguing and delicate life can be. You can also show them practically the differences between plants and how living things interact with the environment.

Let experience be their teacher. When it comes to parenting, this phrase resonates deeply with us. What your child experiences has a greater impact on them than what you tell them about those experiences. Narratives are one-dimensional, but experiences engage almost all the senses. Embrace the opportunity to provide them with as many experiences as possible. These can be planned experiences such as sporting classes at the local community center or impromptu experiences such as purchasing an extra meal and giving it to a person living on the street. Controlled social experiments can help them understand more about their world and what goes on around them.

Experiences that stem from this sort of experiment inspire their curiosity. It leaves a lasting impression and enriches them mentally. This is because the child is involved directly in the process, and reflecting on those experiences develops their analytical thinking skills. These experiments use emotions and feelings, which are very valuable to teachers when it comes to learning. Talking about these experiences creates lasting memories and forms deep and meaningful bonds. There is also a technical aspect, as young children tend to develop an advanced vocabulary to describe the experience and what they are feeling.

Therefore, help them to develop good habits. They say that it takes 21 days to form a new habit. However, life-long habits such as emotional coping mechanisms are formed in this stage. If reading is important to you, then you should read to them and with them. This does not have to be a long time. However, set aside a few minutes each day to read your novel while your child looks at pictures in their favorite book. Children tend to gravitate towards actual pictures in the early part of this stage. Let them look through magazines such as Natural Geographic.

This is also the stage where your children learn about the power of choices. Let them select the material that they look at during this special time. Children should be exposed to various media, including books, magazines, and cartoons. Do not shy away from electronic media. Don't limit their choices just to print media. The objective of this time is to spend time together taking in information. Do not forget those media where we tend not to engage. Sit and listen to different forms of music, such as jazz or ancient music. Remember not to force, but provide opportunities for intimate moments with your child.

Moving is what they do. Children run, jump, and even do more complicated things like hopping on one foot or walking backward. Many children at this stage are already adept at doing flips. Depending on your temperament and that of your child, this could be a source of conflict. A rambunctious child may cause a sedated parent some discomfort. Please resist the urge to restrict their movement. This is one of the ways that children in this stage make sense of their world. If you are worried about your living environment, provide regular opportunities for them to go outside and play. In many communities, there are indoor play areas where children can physically move around in friendly environments.

The tantrums at this stage may not be as feisty as what they displayed during their earlier years, but they are still struggling with expressing their emotions. At this stage, they are only beginning to understand what they feel, but managing those emotions is not yet within their grasp. Part of the problem could be their inability to understand why they feel the way they do fully. Your job as a parent would be to help them process those emotions by giving voice to their thoughts and guiding them on where to concentrate their efforts. However, choose to voice solutions rather than reiterate the problem for a more productive outcome.

No matter how trivial it may seem, like the child's frustration with buttoning their shirt, recognize their frustrations at not being able to do this seemingly simple task. Exercise patience as they try over and over again in a safe and supportive environment. Depending on the level of frustration, you can assist them with the button after you remind them to use their breathing exercises (blowing up their balloons) and then ask them for help. You can then guide them in redirecting their energy to focus on the method of buttoning the shirt.

Don't think that children don't know a lot; in fact, they do. At this age, children are more intellectually developed than many adults realize. They can do simple counting, name colors, and recognize alphabets. Their abilities to perform these things do not just come to them. Like little scientists, they constantly observe, experiment, and assess the outcomes. There will be times that you forget that they are in the room, and you may do or say things that are not appropriate for them to see or hear. You may bang a computer or allow a curse word to escape. Do not become alarmed when you see this behavior in your toddler. Remain calm and have a thoughtful conversation. Do not make excuses or admonish your child to do what you say and not what you do. Apologize for your misstep. Even suggest that you forgot to blow up your balloon and reiterate what you want your child to do if they are in that situation.

Actively empower them. Engaging them in simple problem-solving activities can also help improve their cognitive abilities. Something as little as letting them decide on what activities you will be doing today or what the family will be having for dinner instills a sense of importance. Encourage them to be curious and ask questions. And when providing them with responses, be honest. It is more important for them to think about the question and possible responses than to give them an answer you believe is correct. There will be a natural tendency to shelter your child from difficult discussions. Resist the urge; tell them the truth as you know it, but also encourage them to find their own truth.

These are the formative years of your child so, no matter how busy you are or how tight your budget is, your priority should be to be as present as possible in your child's life. Whether they are just playing, watching TV, or engaged in other experiences, you need to be there with them as much as possible. Time spent with your child does not have to be long or expensive. Your absolute attention for five minutes daily is worth more to your child's development than a trip to an amusement park. As they grow older, it is these memories that the both of you shared in this stage they will remember.

"To be in your children's lives tomorrow ...
you have to be in their lives today."

LIKE WATER FOR CHOCOLATE: AGES 6 TO 10 YEARS

"Whatever you would have your children become,
Try to exhibit in your own lives and conversation"

Lydia H. Sigourney

PREMISES

Late childhood coincides with the school-going years. Children at this age are more physically active than in the early childhood years. They are more involved with friends, and less dependent on parents, and their thinking skills are more complex. Developmental milestones are also more gradual than in the previous stages, even though the changes you see in your child can still be intense.

Children at 6-10 years develop greater muscle strength, coordination, and control, which explains why they will be better at activities already initiated in early childhood, like jumping, throwing, skipping, running, climbing, riding, and kicking a ball. Some may show dexterity in complex skills that require greater muscle coordination, like dancing and skating.

Being good at all these tasks generates a sense of pride and delight and fuels the adventurous nature of this age.

At this age, children dress themselves without any help and move their arms and legs without any effort. By the end of childhood, most children can perform tasks like playing musical instruments as precisely as adults do. A child's brain volume is fully developed by the end of the childhood stage.

However, brain structures continue to define the child's development in cognitive attention, reasoning, and control.

At this stage of cognitive development, children gradually move from the imaginative world of early childhood to become more logical in their thinking. Logic, however, needs to be linked to a concrete reality, so they want to try things for themselves rather than be told how they look, taste, or feel.

By now, they know that there is more than one way of seeing a situation and can consider a problem from different perspectives, which also helps them see other people's point of view. Nonetheless, most of them will consider a single perspective at a time and will still struggle to comprehend how situations are connected. Schoolwork will become lighter for most of them as they have a longer attention span, and the refined coordination of their finer motor skills will allow them to write neatly rather than just print.

Children at the school-going age are more independent from their parents and instead build other relationship bonds with teachers and peers. Friendship and teamwork become extremely important, and acceptance by friends and class groups becomes more emotionally important. Friends of the same sex are more important than those of the opposite sex at this stage. In late childhood, children begin to evaluate their abilities and are aware and sensitive to how others see them. It is now that getting good marks in school begins to matter and can be used to highly or lowly evaluate themselves socially.

They begin to describe themselves and their peers using prevailing social traits like being smart, popular, or mean. Unlike in early childhood, children in late childhood will evaluate their abilities compared to what their peers can do, which can affect their self-esteem and self-concept. Parents of children at this age should understand that their kids need the freedom to explore and grow in a sense of achievement and not be discouraged by too much control. For example, children at this age whose parents perceive their industriousness as mischief may cause them to develop a sense of inferiority.

At this age, children also begin to think about the future and their role in society. They are more conscious about their body as they approach puberty and may start to manifest eating and body image issues in the last years of childhood. They may also experience the pressure to conform to peer styles and ideals.

Late childhood kids are also more conscious of their emotions and have a sense of responsibility for them. They can experience more than one emotion at a time, like being joyful about giving a speech at a school event while at the same time being joyful that they are the chosen one. They are also aware of the situations that elicit their emotions, but they are able to conceal and redirect those emotions, as well as prompt and direct positive emotions to others. At the age of 6-10, children's language and communication skills are more complex and are characterized by more clarity in expression, more complex grammar, and a wider range of vocabulary. Formal instruction transforms and enriches the linguistic input of children at this age and leads them to more excellent linguistic reflection, allowing the development of metalinguistic capacities such as explaining the parts of speech. Their reading and writing skills become more refined, and they can now read with expression and write with greater logic.

Language development for 6-10 year-olds progresses alongside other non-linguistic abilities such as social skills, attention, and memory, depending on the same abilities. For example, children who are more talkative exercise their language skills more, and their increased verbal interaction helps them develop their language more. Similarly, children with a bigger verbal memory capacity will build a richer vocabulary, speak more complex sentences, and retain more words.

Children in this phase of life begin to acquire an intentional dimension, but the intent is selfish rather than altruistic. Doing good for children in this stage is motivated by the personal interest consequences that come out of it. Even when the child seems to act on reciprocity and generosity, the intent is each party's benefit. At this age, children's moral thinking and acting are often guided by philosophies such as "an eye for an eye," "equality" (everybody gets an equal share), "the end justifies the means," and "a favor for a favor."

Children also expect to be rewarded for non-selfish good deeds because the basic moral motivation is the benefit that comes from right acting. Avoiding wrongdoing for children at this stage also has a self-interest end: "don't steal because you'll go to prison," or "don't hit a friend because you'll be left alone without friends."

PERSPECTIVES

Riding the Bus – Tina

It was very important to me to ensure that the children had a sense of independence. We did not want them to depend on others, including us, to determine where they would go or what they would do. Therefore, when Curtis was seven and Nia five, we taught them to use public transportation.

We were living in Ames, Iowa. Ames is a college town, and when we were living there, approximately half of the town was the university population, and approximately half of the town were permanent residents. The city had a very efficient public transportation system. We took advantage of the opportunity to teach the children to ride public transportation while we were attending graduate school.

On Saturday mornings, we would have them walk to the bus stop, which was less than a block from the apartment. They took the bus to the local grocery store, returned glass bottles, and retrieved the deposits. Then they would get back on the bus and ride home. For the first couple of times, I would watch them walk to the bus stop and then trail the bus in the car to ensure that they followed the directions given to them. Then afterwards, they started doing this chore on their own.

Once a week, they took language lessons on the campus. On those days, I would give them bus fare in the morning, and instead of riding the school bus home, they would take the city bus to campus, take their language class and then walk to my office on campus. There was a week when the language classes were canceled, but I forgot to tell the children and did not give them bus fare that morning. That afternoon they showed up at my office. When I asked them what they were doing there, they told me they had gone to their language class, but no one was there. When I asked how they got to campus because I had not given them bus fare, they said they just got on the bus and told the driver that they did not have any money, and because they were little kids, the driver just let them ride.

Teaching Responsibility - George

Early in our marriage, we understood that Tina was better with children while they were younger, and I was better with children at an older age. That is not to say that we would not both be active parents. But ultimately, there would need to be decisions, and there would need to be what came to be called a "primary" parent. Therefore, we decided that Tina would be the primary parent to the children from birth to nine years old, and I would be the primary parent from nine years old to eighteen.

As the primary parent, one of the first things I did was teach the children how to do many household chores. This included shopping for groceries. The kids would go through the kitchen and make a grocery list. I would drive them to the grocery store, sit at the front, and read. They would push the buggy through the grocery store gathering items from the list. I would meet them at the register and write a check for the items. When we got home, they would put the food away. It wasn't long before I noticed that the grocery bill was getting higher and higher. It was then I noticed all of the snack items that were not on the grocery list that somehow ended up in the grocery cart. This was the time for the conversation about the difference between needs and wants.

Communicating Responsibility – Tina

When the children were young, we still had home telephones that everyone in the house used. We made it a point to allow the children to answer the phone when they were very young. Because we moved from Florida to Iowa then, they were used to talking to relatives by phone since we lived so far from family. Although they knew how to talk on the phone, we taught them to answer the phone in a specific way. They answered the phone with, "Hello, Bradley residence." We taught them that when they called someone, they should greet the person on the line, announce who they were by stating their name, and then they were to state their business.

When we transitioned to mobile phones, we also bought phones for the children. The phones were so that the children could communicate with us or others who were in charge of transporting them to extracurricular activities or watching them when we were on travel. There were many times when we had to travel at the last minute or had not properly communicated with each other, and we would not be home with the children. We would call them to let them know what they were supposed to do, who would be transporting them to their extracurricular activities, or who would stay with them overnight.

When the children were in middle school, they attended a laboratory school on a college campus. The school was supposed to employ the most innovative practices based on contemporary education research. However, we found that it was a typical school with very little innovation at all. The school had been given a lot of money to develop its technology infrastructure. As a part of that infrastructure development, all students were assigned a laptop. This was during a time when every child having a laptop that the school assigned was just becoming popular. It is interesting to note that twenty years later, one can still hear teachers and parents talking about schools assigning students laptops as an innovative practice. The year that laptops were given to all middle school students in this laboratory school, Nia was in the sixth grade.

During the parent orientation, I was shocked and appalled at some of the policies that were put in place regarding the laptops. A lot of emphasis was placed on the casing of the selected laptops to ensure that students did not destroy them. There was no mention of school personnel actively teaching students how to care for the devices. When each teacher explained how they were going to use the laptop as a part of their instruction, the English teacher indicated that no student would be able to use the laptop in her class until the student could demonstrate that they could type a certain number of words per minute with a minimum number of errors. Copies of all of the students' textbooks were loaded to the hard drive of every computer.

The school decided to disable the feature that would allow the laptops to connect to the internet. In fact, when representatives from one of the agencies who sponsored the laptop project came to see how they were being used, the school loaded several web pages on each laptop and had the students toggle between those pages as if they were searching the web during the visit by the government officials.

During this time, we actively taught Curtis and Nia how to use technologies responsibly. We purposely worked with them when we were introduced to new information. While they were still in middle school, we would articulate ideas or challenges, and they would make technology recommendations to address the issues.

PROMISES

This is the point in a child's life where you sit back and marvel at the progress that they have made. Every achievement they make or milestone they cross feels like a personal achievement for you. And many parents tend to personalize their children's victories or perceived failures, which has its own consequences. We see many parents posting their children's accomplishments and triumphs on social media. There is nothing wrong with this, to a certain degree. Your child's growth and development is not about you. Each child will develop in their own time. It is your responsibility to provide opportunities for them to spread their wings, fall, and get back up again in a safe and loving environment.

This is the stage at which many parents delegate much of their children's guidance to others. This is typically when children go to a formal school, and parents lean heavily on teachers and school systems to provide guidance for their children. Many conscientious parents believe that moving to a particular neighborhood where schools have better reputations is how to plan for their children purposefully. The development of children goes beyond their cognitive development.

As a parent, it is your hope that you have adequately prepared your child for this stage of learning. Hopefully, you have done some research on the school you would like them to attend long before now. If not, get into it right away. Find a school that provides a safe and conducive environment for learning. The principles and values they teach in the school should build on the foundations you have already laid in the child's life. There are bound to be some differences because the school brings together students from different backgrounds, and the teachers and the administrative staff also share in this diversity. For some parents, this might be a concern. When my husband and I decided on the school that my children will attend, many factors went into the decision-making process, and we will discuss them in detail in the perspective section. Essentially, you may have to make some compromises.

Your job does not end with conducting school searches and then doing pickups and drop-offs. Your child's education is not something you simply hand off to someone else, even if the person is an expert. You have to play an active role in this journey. It is important to build a good relationship with your child's teacher. This opens the door for communication so that your concerns about your child's learning progress can be expressed to the teacher and vice versa. Following this, you are to ensure that your child does their homework on time. They may need your input in certain areas, so plan to be there for them. Being hands-on in helping your child with their schoolwork at home can improve their learning and performance in school. And this is the ultimate goal you should strive for.

There are many areas that you need to consider as your child moves through formal school. However, given the interdependence in the world, individuals who speak more than one language are at an advantage. For most schools, serious formal language studies start in middle or high school, whereas the optimal time to learn a second language starts much earlier in a child's life. Speaking multiple languages not only opens up opportunities as they grow older but also changes how your child's brain works, making them better in analytical thinking, multitasking, and problem-solving. All of this makes them better prepared as they move through the world.

For the child, this is the time to dream. We have always been very emphatic in our views that a child's dreams do not have to be influenced by their area codes, the social status of their parents, or their health condition. Whether they live in the slums or a highbrow area of the society, their dreams can take them out and above their environment. There are many success stories that have proven this. These real-life stories feature different backgrounds, different experiences, and different cultures. But they have one common thread. Their dreams and ambitions were nurtured by someone they were close to. In some cases, it was a parent, grandparent, or a close aunt. For others, it was someone they were unrelated to, like a neighbor or a coach. These people recognized the potential in that child and actively steered them towards actualizing their goals.

Being a parent, you can decide to be the nurturer of your child's dreams. Recognize their talent, help them hone their abilities, invest in those talents and most importantly, push them to aspire for more. It is not always as easy as it sounds when you look at how we listed everything. To support your child's dreams may take sacrifices from you long before your child begins to make those sacrifices themselves. But it is always worth it when your efforts pay out in the end.

You also become the protector of your child's dreams as others try to limit your child's potential to do whatever they have decided to do. Many adults in your child's life have been professionally trained to work with children. The work of teachers, coaches, and other professionals are generally not designed to promote independent thought and innovative actions. Schools are complex environments that are generally focused on order and are not places for the messiness that typically accompanies divergent thought. It is up to parents to protect their children's thoughts and dreams. Children should be reminded that dreams can be frightening. In fact, if their dreams don't terrify them, they are probably not dreaming big enough.

Encourage your children to open their minds. Making sure they are exposed to as much as possible helps them believe that they can accomplish anything and that anything is possible. All types of excursions, day trips, and vacations are important. Trips don't have to be expensive. Trips to different parts of the neighborhood in your town can be made into an adventure. By taking your children to a playground across town, they can see different aspects of the community and possibly meet different friends. Also, look for opportunities sponsored by non-profit organizations in your area.

For parents who like to think that they are very practical in their approach to doing things, it may be difficult to marry dreams with reality, especially when there is a stark contrast between the two. There is nothing wrong with maintaining a firm grasp of reality—at least not until your grip begins to hold your child back in areas where they are supposed to make advancements. If nothing else, dreams are one of the most powerful tools that can be used to teach a child how to be responsible for their choices instead of taking life's hits and being victims of circumstances.

Help children identify their strengths and identify those resources that will support them to make their dreams come true. For instance, a child who dreams of becoming an artist but shows no natural talent should be enrolled in art classes, introduced to artists, and attend art shows to support them in developing skills and inspiration to support their dreams. Focus should be placed on the process instead of the result. The key to identifying their strengths is encouraging them to follow their passion. Where there is passion, there is will, which is an important ingredient for success.

Self-Efficacy

Not enough can be said about promoting self-efficacy in your children. Insisting that they make their bed, pick up after themselves, and washing their clothes is not just supporting the work of a busy family. Giving children responsibilities builds a sense of self-worth and character that will benefit them through adulthood. Self-efficacy is a precursor to responsibility. With focus on the person they would become, teaching self-efficacy should be less about chores and more about activities that build their characters. That is not to say chores are not to be treated with priority. If you have already started the children on routine chores, stick with it and increase their responsibilities as they grow. If you haven't, you should get started right away.

Financial literacy should be encouraged. Money matters are serious matters, but do not have to be complex for children at this stage. Children don't have to earn money to understand the value of it. Getting first-hand experience with managing finances will set them on the right path to engage confidently with money in the future successfully. Financial education at this stage should include being accountable with money, being conscious of the value of money, and having healthy habits related to money.

Social graces will take them far. Social engagements should include spending time with individuals in their age group, along with individuals who are older and younger individuals than they are. Social graces go beyond general good manners. Children should be encouraged to challenge society's status quo and think about positive social change. Don't be afraid to support your children's thoughts about complex topics. If they are old enough to ask the question, your response should focus on your children engaging with information to develop their thoughts and ideas instead of promoting your ideas about the subject.

Focus on experiences as opposed to a means to an end. Community parenting involves using the resources in your environment to support your child's growth. Our definition of community parenting is supporting parents' work whether you are related to the individual or not. It can also be maintained that community parenting involves using other adults in the community to expose children to individuals with specialized skills. Community parenting is what many coaches and counselors in the community do as they focus on helping young people grow and develop. It is also taking advantage of older members of the community as a way of making history come alive.

Create healthy eating habits combined with a lifestyle that incorporates physical exercise. The little seeds you sow today could help your child form habits that would promote a healthy lifestyle.

1. Model the behavior you expect. You would have to model the behavior you want your child to emulate. If you eat healthy, chances are they would do the same too. If you exercise regularly, they may want to partake in it too.

2. Reduce the amount of sugar in their diet. This can be done by adding more live food—fruits and vegetables. This does not mean that treats are completely off-limits. As with everything else, balance is key.

3. Instead of dictating the menu, offer a variety of healthy food options to choose from. This makes mealtime more fun.

4. Exercises at this stage should be more fun and games than adults' strict exercise regimen. Activities like swimming, dancing, and playing games outside naturally involve full body workouts.

5. Do things together by making them team players. Children at this stage are more likely to get involved if everyone else in the family is doing it. Add a walk around the neighborhood after the whole family shares at least one meal together. This strengthens bonds and promotes mental health.

Your child's interest when it comes to technology gradually shifts from the regular children's games and educational materials to socializing. Sure, they still use the internet to conduct research for school-related work and still play games, but you would find that they are doing a lot of interacting with their peers. However, their peers are not the only ones trying to socialize with your child. There are predators actively searching for victims. There is also tons of inappropriate content that your child can access out of curiosity or at the nudging of others.

Then there is also the possibility of your child getting obsessively attached to addictive video games. Besides setting up internet safety measures with parental control, here are a few things you can do to ensure that they don't get stuck in the swirly world of technology;

1. Set a time limit for tech usage. They should have a scheduled time for using technology for their homework and also for some leisure time in between. Also, ensure that the technology is used in the right place. For instance, there should be no technology during meal times or when they are in the bathroom. You should also endeavor to model this behavior even as you enforce it.

2. Video games and social media interactions should be interspersed with physical games and interactions with real people. There should be more of the latter.

3. It is important that you are selective of the kinds of platforms your child is on and the kind of video games they play, especially at this stage.

4. Educate yourself on the technology being used. It feels like every other day, a new technology springs up. Leaving your child to figure it out on their own can open the door for them to be exploited. Consider learning the technology with your child; allowing your child to teach you can be very empowering.

5. Keep your child's information safe. There has been an increase in identity theft cases thanks to the carelessness of children with their personal information. Educate them on the importance of keeping those details to themselves. Even disclosing their location could compromise their safety.

Children grow up fast. One minute, you are singing them to sleep; the next, they are having sleepovers with friends. One day, they are sitting on a highchair at the dining table; the next, they are making the meals you serve. These are probably the last years of their childhood.

Enjoy each moment. Don't be in a hurry to have them grow up. Let these moments linger for as long as possible. Encourage playtime. The phrase "let them be children" should be a daily mantra this season. While you try to teach your child all the other things essential for their development, give them moments to run around, get their clothes dirty, play in the rain, etc. Of course, they have to clean up after themselves after they have had all the fun, but the important thing is that they have fun amidst all the seriousness.

Every parent should have a journal where you can write down memorable experiences you had with the children. If you are not the writing kind, you can create a scrapbook or a memory jar that collects bits and pieces that remind you of special moments. Better still, put your inner photographer to work. It is not about getting the perfect shot, writing eloquently, or looking for that special piece. It is about capturing the moments, treasuring them, and most importantly, being present because this is what they would remember at the end of the day.

"The way we talk to children becomes their inner voice"

-Peggy O'Mara

THE JOY LUCK CLUB: AGES 11 – 18

"It seems I have officially lost my mind.
I think my children ran away with it ..."

Unknown

PREMISES

When thinking of parenting a teenager, the image of a headless chicken running around comes to mind. That paints a gruesome picture, but you would be surprised by how accurate this description is. There are a lot of things that occur in this stage that make you feel like you are losing your mind. In this stage, you can say goodbye to that sweet, adorable child with eyes that beamed like the sun; the baby you used to know and say hello to this feisty temperamental individual whom you know you share some sort of genetic relationship with. But you just don't recognize this new person.

It will not be all war and battle of wills as you will catch glimpses of the child you once knew in there. Good for you if you happen to have a teenager who is pretty much still the children from the previous years despite the physical changes. But brace yourself for moments when the rebel within shows up. This is not always an outright rebellion.

This is another growth spurt stage, which happens just in time for puberty. For the girls, their breasts start to develop, they begin their menstrual cycle, and their hair starts growing in under their arms, in their pubic region, and on their arms and legs. Their hips may begin to expand also. For boys, they may start growing hair on their face and chest, arms, and genital area. Their voice changes, becoming deeper in tone, and their muscles may start to become more defined. Some children may experience certain pains because of the rapid growth of their bodies during this time.

At this stage, their emotional development revolves around finding their place in this world. At this point, children try to fill what they feel is lacking in their relationships at home with their relationships with other people. They may seem selfish at this point, but it is not because they want to be malicious in their quest to meet their needs. They are just really into finding answers to questions around their identity. They start to wonder about their faith, their beliefs, and even you; their parents will not escape their questioning. They may not come outright to ask those questions, but even when they do, your answers may not be entirely satisfactory for them. Teens may do a lot more exploring. There are many good sides to this explorative side of them, but it also has its downfall. For starters, teens are more vulnerable to the manipulative behaviors of others. This vulnerability plays out in their real relationships and virtual ones too.

Although teens are mostly into themselves, they can actually understand the ideas and feelings of people around them. They show some amount of empathy because of this growing ability. They understand broader concepts of morality. If exposed to global issues, they may be able to formulate their own opinion on these issues and take a stand. Before they turn 18, they may not be legally permitted to do much, but they would be willing to partake in activities supporting their beliefs. Because they are doing a lot of exploring in this phase, some of their choices may be poor. But their brains and minds are developed enough to learn from their mistakes.

The lines between good, bad, and the gray areas are becoming clearer for your teenager. By the time they get to

18, they can understand abstract concepts like morality. That is not to say that they didn't know morals before this age. The difference is that morality during the younger years was more about their feelings and emotions, and then as they grow older, they start thinking of it as rules and instructions that they have to obey. By the time they get to seven, they know that actions have consequences, and they have a sense of fairness. Now, they recognize and respect the rules but also want to navigate them by negotiating. Rules are no longer blindly accepted. They want to understand the whys of it, and oftentimes, if the rules conflict with their desire to explore, they may want to bend it a bit. That 9 p.m. curfew might stretch for an additional hour.

Your teenager may have more bluff than actual confidence at this point. For all their bravado, they are very emotionally vulnerable. Trying to deal with the physical and hormonal changes in their body is both terrifying and exciting at the same time. These changes can cause an identity crisis. And when they begin to question who they are, it can affect their confidence. To boost their confidence, they begin affiliating themselves with objects, people, or habits that they think would make them appear "cool."

Essentially, their confidence in this stage is not drawn from the inside of them, which is the roots you have tried to establish all these years. Rather, it feeds off the opinions of others. This is why they may begin to think that being friends with the most famous person in school might help, or wearing the latest designer clothes, or driving the latest cars might help boost confidence. Given what they are going through, it is easy to understand how they may want to lean on others for support.

You can help them get their power back by building a healthy foundation for their confidence. Having a few likes and comments on your social media posts is great, but letting your happiness and joy hang on that is like taking a speed jet to poor self-esteem. Teach them that superficial things like these cannot replace their values and self-worth. Let your teen be free to make their choices, but balance that freedom with guidance. Most importantly, you have to model the kind of confidence you want to see in them.

If your child's fussiness with their dressing in their previous years drove you nuts, it is going to be nothing compared to what your appearance-conscious teen would become. And this is not gender specific. Sure, the girls would have their endless hours of makeup, and the boys would be fiddling with their thin facial hair, but the same level of attention is given to their appearance.

Right about now, the initial curious interest in the opposite sex your child had in the earlier years develops into a full-fledged sexual interest. And given their predisposition to exploring new things, you better believe that exploring their interest in the opposite sex would be very high on their agenda. This is not something any parent wants to deal with, but it is a reality you are going to have to accept. The best you can do is ensure that your teen is provided with the right kind of sexual information that would enable them to make the right choices.

Remember that gaming thing we talked about earlier? They are going to be doing a lot of it now. It can get frustrating, especially for the boys, so you might as well get used to it. Girls are not so much into video games, but their social interests could leave you with brow-raising phone bills at the end of the month. You are going to have to set limits. Between their blossoming personalities, crazy new habits, and raging hormones, you might find yourself running around the house like the headless chicken mentioned earlier as you try to establish order. It won't be easy and certainly won't look like it, but this too shall pass.

Teens encouraged to actively pursue projects they care about are usually passionately involved in activities supporting their cause around this age. Their abilities to think beyond themselves and empathize with others enhance this kind of thinking. This is the other side of those selfish teenage tendencies we talked about. It enables them fully to commit to what they care about, and if the community falls within that purview, you would be amazed at the lengths your teen would go to instigate a change.

Social responsibility requires one to think of others; for teenagers, this can largely provide answers to some of the questions they are struggling with. Their community involvement would be determined by the foundations they lay. But it doesn't end with you. Many schools these days are initiating projects that teach service learning, while some even make it mandatory with certain programs that have community service as a requirement. Participating in school fundraisers or simply volunteering to donate blood are just some of the things they can do. If your teen is politically inclined, they might use their voices in advocacy groups.

All of this is good for your teen as it helps build their confidence and makes them feel accepted as a part of their community. It also reflects positively on their resume and college applications. And because being socially responsible might require them to interact with peers and adults outside the typical sphere of influence, they would be able to build new relationships. For optimal results, be sure that the social projects your teen is involved in are something that they genuinely care about. It matters to them when they see that regardless of what is going on, they have the power to make a difference.

These are some of the most exciting and terrifying years of a teen's life. Amid the active social life, there is serious academic work going on. Homework is now more complex, and there will be a lot of projects that require some planning if your teen is to make good grades. These are the years for you and your child to plan for college, even though it is still a few years away. The school will offer several course choices. Encourage your child to take more challenging school work like advanced placement (AP) courses later in their years. It might require extra study hours and more effort, but it goes a long way to cementing their future with a good university if they can get good grades. Those good grades would earn them extra credit.

Of course, there are going to be the courses they like, the ones they dislike, and then those other mandatory subjects. The goal is to have a balanced educational experience. They would have to take their study game up a notch to cope with these new classes, especially when there are many extracurricular activities that help build character but can also serve as a distraction. All of the stress of taking new courses, participating in new activities, and also keeping an active social life could lead to eating and sleeping disorders. Some teens in this condition might be susceptible to coping mechanisms that have adverse effects, such as drugs and alcohol. As your teen strives for academic excellence, it is your job to ensure that they have a healthy balance in all their school activities. Ensure that they are eating well and getting enough sleep.

PERSPECTIVES

Responsibility - George

We moved around a lot while rearing the children. If we got an offer for a position or opportunity, then we would move the family. Where the children were in their development or what they were doing was only a part of our decision-making process. Right before Curtis's sophomore year, we moved from Orangeburg, South Carolina, to Summerville, South Carolina, because we both got new positions. I gave Curtis the opportunity to stay in Orangeburg. He would live with his grandmother and continue to attend the high school where he was enrolled. Curtis said that he wanted to stay. When asked why he wanted to stay, Curtis said he did not want to leave his friends. I knew that this was not a sound reason for making this decision, and I decided that Curtis would come to Summerville with the rest of the family.

Curtis played on the junior varsity football team during his first year in Orangeburg. His career there was unremarkable. When we moved to Summerville, Curtis tried out and made the junior varsity football team. The varsity coaches sent for him and asked him to try out for varsity. Curtis was evidently a very talented player who had not been challenged. He started on the varsity team at Summerville in his sophomore year. That team would win the state championship that year.

During his junior year, he racked up all kinds of awards not only in football, but also in wrestling and track. I think that because of his newfound acclaim, teachers also started paying more attention to him. He was exposed to various opportunities and experiences to include being recommended for advanced placement (AP) courses even though his grades were only average. He represented Summerville High School at Boys State and spent the summer between his junior and senior year in high school in Costa Rica as a part of a study abroad program offered by the University of Oregon.

At the end of Curtis's junior year of high school, Tina and I received new and exciting opportunities that would require me to be based in Columbia and travel throughout the state. Tina's new position would be at a college in Columbia, South Carolina. We thought about what we should do with Curtis.

We really thought that if we decided to move him during his senior year, the Summerville community would put hits out on our lives. Curtis and the rest of the Summerville football team had become more or less local heroes. When they went to local restaurants, little children would request their autographs. I held a membership at the local golf club. One weekend I called to get a tee time and was told that they were booked for the weekend. Curtis called right afterwards and was told that they would make a spot for the "number one offensive lineman in the state."

As we considered moving to Columbia, I asked Curtis what he wanted to do. He said he wanted to complete his senior year at Summerville. I made the decision to rent a small two-bedroom apartment in Summerville, where Curtis would live during his senior year in high school. It was not a difficult decision to make. Curtis had always been a responsible person. His sensibilities were always a little beyond his age. Very few people outside the immediate family knew that Curtis was staying alone. He always told his friends that he and I lived in the apartment. When his friends came over, and I was not there, Curtis would tell them that I was away on a business trip.

There was not a lot of discussion about rules and behavior. The only thing that I told Curtis is that if there was any trouble and something did go wrong, we would have him live with one of my cousins. There were a lot of children in that home, and he would not have the kind of privacy that he had grown accustomed to.

Curtis completed his senior year without incident. During the last week of school, he held a party at the apartment, where his friends finally figured out that he was living alone. By then, he was planning to pack up the apartment and prepare himself for college. When people asked us how we could leave a 17-year-old in an apartment by themselves, I reminded them that in a few months, he would not only be 18 years old, but he would also be living on his own in someone's residence hall on someone's campus and thus needed to learn how to govern himself at some time.

The Role of Sports – George

Sports were always extracurricular activities for both of the children. I always felt that playing and engaging in athletics gave them an opportunity to learn certain concepts that they would see later in life. They would learn to practice something, interact with people of their age, and form relationships with adults other than their family or teachers. Sports, to me, is a microcosm of life.

Nia's talent seemed to be more about academics. She did play tennis in high school. I watched her play basketball with certain family members. Her game was okay, but I never expected her to play organized basketball. Curt first played baseball, and I always thought baseball was one of his better sports. He always loved basketball, but he was only fair at it. He was not a bad basketball player, and he had decent moves. He loved to play because basketball was the sport that most of the family played. Most of his cousins and uncles and the community played basketball. Because of his size and a lot of peer pressure from the community and the school, I feel that he ventured into the areas of athletics that he did—track, wrestling, and football.

I was always saddened that Curt never had an opportunity to finish out baseball. However, there was a lot of pressure to specialize. Additionally, when he was in school, the seasons of each sport overlapped, and it would have been difficult for him to play baseball and football. By the end of his senior year, he had won championships in all three sports he participated in.

I thought that participating in various sports just made individuals well-rounded. While Nia selected a sport she would play beyond high school, Curt's sports would not continue into adulthood. While we were living in Summerville, Curt became interested in playing golf. I wanted him to learn to play because it was for us to bond. Golf was a sport that we could play together where we could talk and hang out.

I never received any training in golf, and Curtis wanted me to teach him. I understood one thing about athletics: if you do not learn the fundamentals, you'll be stuck with bad form. I hired a professional to teach Curtis golf. He learned the mechanics, and to this day he's an excellent golfer. We still play a lot. I still have the same terrible game I had back then, but was wise enough not to pass on all those bad habits to my son.

We only had one rule regarding sports. If the children started a sport, they couldn't quit when things did not go their way. They had to take it to its logical conclusion. They had to learn to deal with those trials and tribulations if something didn't go their way. I knew those were the same things they would deal with in life.

School Choice – Tina

We were in the process of looking for a home and deciding where Nia would finish high school when we relocated to Columbia, South Carolina. We had lived in Columbia before and knew the reputation of the schools in the area. I also worked for a college where the president was given a voucher to send their high school-aged children to any school in the city. When he asked why he would not send his children to the school where they were zoned, he was told that the schools were not very good.

He and his wife decided to send their children to one of the schools with a better reputation than the neighborhood school. When the mother went to register the children for school, a district administrator pulled her to the side and suggested that the neighborhood school would be the better choice. She took his advice and was glad that she did. Not only did their children do well in high school, they became extremely successful professionals.

We agreed with that philosophy and purchased a home in an older neighborhood where the city was trying to attract families with diverse incomes. The house was within walking distance from the predominantly African American school where we wanted Nia to attend. However, we would later find out that the house was zoned for a school with one of the best reputations in the city and the state. We had already decided that Nia would attend the neighborhood school with a bad reputation.

Our decision to send her to the school in the first place was because of the small class sizes. The class size at the school averaged eight students to one teacher. Unfortunately, this was not by design. The class sizes were so small because most of the families who could send their children to another school did. Only the children of families in the community who may not have had the resources to send their children to other places remained.

For Nia to attend the school, we had to apply for out-of-zone placement. When people found out what we were doing, everyone from distant family members to people we barely knew to the school district personnel in charge of processing our application for out-of-zone placement actively encouraged us to reconsider. A family member reported that they served as a substitute teacher in the neighborhood school and that the children were out of control. The person in charge of processing our application for out-of-zone placement stated that the application would be approved if there was an available room at the school. We knew that there was room at the school because there were constant stories in the media of closing the school because of low enrollment.

After a lot of discouragement, we were given out-of-zone placement. Nia went on to attend the school and have several high school experiences that would have been very difficult for us to create had she gone to any other school. By examining the type of person Nia was at that time and the person we wanted her to become, we selected a school environment that helped us as we worked with her through her high school experience.

A Service Orientation – George

We have always believed in children having a service orientation. We looked for opportunities for the children to provide service. Not only did we feel that their activity would benefit individuals in their community, but the learning experiences provided were not things we could replicate in the formal school environment.

Our first effort to provide Curtis and Nia with a volunteer experience failed. We wanted them to volunteer in a home for the elderly that was within walking distance of their school. Our purpose for attempting to set up this experience was that our parents were fairly young grandparents, and the children did not have much experience around individuals who were very old. We wanted them to read the newspaper or Bible to individuals who lived in the home. However, we could not convince the administrative staff to allow the children to do this project.

We decided to pull them into the work that we were doing on a college campus. When I was asked as a college administrator to speak in a class or to a community group, and my schedule would not allow it, I would provide Curtis with the information, and he would give the speech for me. We were committed to having the children engage with adults in other environments. We were fortunate enough to move to a community where the hospital had a volunteer program for young people. The training program involved an interview and training process, which was great practice for interviews that they would have for college admission and internships. We thought that they would be working in the gift shop delivering gifts to patient's rooms. To our surprise, Curtis worked transporting patients and delivering items to the emergency room.

In high school, Nia did not want to take art or music as an elective. She found a course on community service in the high school catalog and asked to take it. When she was told that the course was not offered because there wasn't a teacher to teach it, she spoke to the director of the local community center about an idea to teach elementary school students computer skills. We helped her write a proposal to the high school administration. I attended the meeting with her to ensure that the adults did not ignore her idea. They had the right to turn her down, but I wanted to ensure they took her efforts seriously. They approved her proposal, and she went on to recruit some of her high school colleagues to work with her to teach elementary school students computer skills at the community center.

Children of The World – Tina

As a high school student, I was concerned about the fact that Curtis was learning Spanish II from a person who did not have Spanish language skills. I wanted him to be able to communicate in Spanish. I looked for a Spanish immersion program but never found one. Curtis identified a summer study abroad program sponsored by the University of Oregon in Costa Rica. It was mad expensive, but we had to find a way for him to participate. George took an extra job, and Curtis enrolled in the program.

Curtis spent the summer of his junior year of high school in Costa Rica. Although the outcome of language learning was not achieved, he had a good cultural exchange. He met different people and had different experiences. I think most of his engagement was with other American students on the trip. But there were opportunities to engage with Costa Rican families. There were also excursions to the rainforest and discussions of endangered species. These are things that he could have read about in a book. I am so glad that he got these experiences firsthand. I would like to think that this experience helped to shape how he sees himself in the world.

Not one to let her brother do more than she does, Nia traveled to Brazil for her sophomore year in high school through Rotary International. Like her brother's experience, Nia's experience set her on a trajectory of being a true citizen of the world. Traveling and experiencing different parts of the world is a critical part of how she sees herself.

Unlike her brother, she did master Portuguese and has retained her language skills. She traveled all over Brazil and had amazing experiences, from swimming in the Amazon River to dancing with indigenous peoples. Her colleagues were from all over the world, and she still communicates with friends from Brazil, South Africa, and Japan.

People asked us how we could consider sending our 15-year-old daughter to Brazil unaccompanied. George and I both had the same reaction … how could we not?

PROMISES

Life with your teen is interesting and amazing. If you have cultivated your relationship with your child through the years, their teen years will be so rewarding to you. Even with the changes that are taking place with them physically and emotionally, they will always return to the center if you have developed a healthy relationship.

Many things have changed but are still very much the same. This means that your relationship with them has evolved. When they were younger, they wanted you to come into their room to play or read their favorite bedtime stories. As they try on independence, they may be less willing to spend as much time and personal space with you.

It may seem that they are pushing away from you, and it can be a very confusing time for you and your child. It is important to walk a fine line between respecting their right to privacy and being vigilant enough to ensure they are safe. They are more vulnerable at this stage than perhaps at any other stage in their lives. Yet on the outside, they act tough and may act as if they understand everything in the world.

As unnerving as this can be, this is also the time when you can have the most meaningful conversations with your child, learn about the person they are becoming, and practice allowing them to express their thoughts and ideas without judgment.

Adolescence is an interesting period in human development. In terms of cognitive skills, individuals should have mastered all the basic skills needed to function as educated individuals. Mathematically, they would be able to add, subtract, multiply and divide, which is all that one can do with numbers. Therefore, they are now able to apply advanced mathematical concepts such as algebra, trigonometry, geometry, and statistics. They would have completely mastered speaking at least one language and could use that language to communicate with others in writing. All of the other skills are areas that need to be practiced, honed, and fine-tuned well into adulthood.

Since we live in the age of information, the idea that formal school is the only way for individuals to acquire new knowledge and skills is a flawed notion. With information literally at one's fingertips, the purpose of formal education is more complex and provides adolescents to develop social-emotional and critical thinking skills as well as habits of mind.

Starting in elementary school but carrying on through high school, students should practice:

- **Self-awareness**—accurately assessing one's feelings, interests, values, and strengths; maintaining a well-grounded sense of self-confidence.

- **Self-management**—regulating one's emotions to handle stress, control impulses, and persevere in overcoming obstacles; setting and monitoring progress toward personal and academic goals; expressing emotions appropriately.

- **Social awareness**—being able to take the perspective of and empathize with others; recognizing and appreciating individual and group similarities and differences; recognizing and using family, school, and community resources.

- **Relationship skills**—establishing and maintaining healthy and rewarding relationships based on cooperation; resisting inappropriate social pressure; preventing, managing, and resolving interpersonal conflict; seeking help when needed.

- **Responsible decision-making**—making decisions based on consideration of ethical standards, safety concerns, appropriate social norms, respect for others, and likely consequences of various actions; applying decision-making skills to academic and social situations; contributing to the well-being of one's school and community.

Schools should be places where individuals can practice these skills with individuals of similar ages. Unfortunately, in most schools, there remains a focus on teaching core subjects as opposed to helping students learn through all disciplines. It is important that teens practice these extremely useful skills and learn about themselves.

Even though schools are not engaged in this work, parents can support their teens' development of these skills by involving them in real-world activities. Don't forget to look at things that are in your environment. If you work in construction, involve your teen in work like cleaning up the site or updating spreadsheets in the office. If you work as a nurse, speak with the talent specialists in your organizations about opportunities for your teen to deliver flowers from the gift shop to patients' rooms or provide visitors to the hospital with directions. It is important that your children volunteer for these positions. Those positions where teens are paid tend not to be positions where they can acquire the best skills.

Young people are resilient. We have heard stories from families who did not move because their child was at a certain age—usually in high school—and the family did not want to disturb their progress. Human beings have the enormous capacity to adapt. Flexibility is one of the most important skills for individuals to have. In fact, flexibility is a skill that is critically important because life offers so many changes that are beyond our control. From environmental changes brought on by global warming to global pandemics that disrupt our lives, the only constant in life is change. Young people are more than capable of handling these changes if they just see them as a part of life. Support your teen as they embrace changes as a natural part of life. Welcome the changes and see the good in things that may occur in their lives.

Communication is the key to any relationship. There are three elements of communication. The first is the verbal message, which includes the words you choose to use. The second, the paraverbal message, denotes how you use the words. And lastly, the nonverbal message is portrayed more in our body language.

Take a deep breath before communicating, especially if your emotions are running high and you need to communicate with your child. The simple act of filling your lungs with air and slowly releasing it does absolute wonders for the way you feel and the way your brain functions. Make sure to take a moment to breathe before responding to situations with your teen that could lead to conflict. Sometimes you will need to take two breaths.

Always learn to listen. According to Will Schwalbe, *"The greatest gift that you can give anyone is your undivided attention."* As a part of the communication process, we spend more time learning how to make a point than we do practicing the skill of listening. Listening is an extremely important skill in the communication process. You may believe that you are hearing what your teen is saying at times, but you must understand and learn to listen to what they are attempting to communicate to you. Your teen has a lot to say and may not be using the right words to express themselves. If you do not have good listening skills, you will never figure out what they are attempting to convey, nor will you give them the time to communicate the best way that they can. Listening is more than just talking less. Paying attention to their body language, moods and even what they are not saying is key to understanding what they are trying to convey.

More important than what you are saying back to your teen, just listening to them without responding can be more powerful than any words of wisdom you can provide. Practicing active listening without responding back empowers your teen to trust themselves and their decision-making. If you must respond, you should practice asking probing questions to ensure you understand before responding. A good practice is to articulate back to them what you think you heard to ensure that you understand.

Avoid prying. As a parent, you want to get answers immediately and may be tempted to ask direct confrontational questions. Teens are more likely to share information with you if they don't feel pressured. Resist the urge to push for answers. Give your teen the space to share information with you. Remember to be a good steward of that information. What is given to you in confidence should be kept in confidence. Maintain your child's trust unless they are threatening themselves or others. Check your behavior. Your children will follow your lead if you continue to model good judgment and behavior. If you see your child engaging in inappropriate behavior, the first person you should look at is yourself—not your spouse, their friends, the television, or any other entity beyond your control. The only person you can control is yourself.

Make sure that what you are doing supports what you want your child to do. Children tend to do what we do, not what we say. Make sure that your behavior is in line with what you expect from your child. Children are always watching you. You must strike a balance between your actions and your words. Allow both to align. They know and see things that you wouldn't think that they see, and they understand at a very early age. Never underestimate the brilliance of children. Always check your behavior.

Embrace mistakes. As long as you are living, you will make mistakes. It is through mistakes that we learn. What is important is what you do after you have made a mistake. When you have made a mistake and have taken ownership for the mistake, take the opportunity to talk to your children about those mistakes and what you learned. Your children will learn that lapses in judgment are a part of being human. Encourage your children to practice forgiving themselves and learning from their mistakes.

If by chance your behavior is not stellar, admit the inappropriate action, and discuss with your teen what you should have done. Remember to apologize in the same manner you exhibited the inappropriate behavior. If you yell at a salesperson in a store at a level where others can hear, make sure that you apologize in a manner where others around can hear.

Don't be dismissive of your children's experiences. You may hear dramatic declarations like, "if I don't have that shirt, I am going to die," and be tempted to brush off this exaggeration. If you want to foster communication with your teen, you will have to dig in to reconnect with the teenager in you and show some empathy for what they are going through. If you are not that type of teenager, this is a good time to try to get to know your child. Separate the drama from the intent of the message and encourage clear and informed communication. Be able to articulate the rationale for your decision. And remember that all emotions are a part of the human experience, even disappointment.

Do stuff together. Communication isn't always about talking. You can schedule weekly or bi-monthly activities that feature different family configurations. One child and all adults, one child and one adult, all children and one adult, all children and all adults. Choose activities of interest and do them together. Let one person select an activity and engage. Remember that it is important to give as much respect to the activity selected by the child as you give an activity selected by the adult. If you want your child to respect things in your life, you must model that respect for things that they value.

Never underestimate the power of a shared meal. With busy lives that are led by all, it may be difficult to share meals consistently. Try to set one meal where everything stops except the sharing of the meal. This could be Tuesday dinner, Saturday breakfast, or Sunday brunch. If time and interest permit, consider adding the meal's preparation to this activity. Assign different members the responsibility for preparing the meals. If your family is competitive, create competitions. A consistent routine will not only allow for engagement but also set up an opportunity to create a tradition or build a memory. Try to maintain the regular family routine of having dinner together.

We have talked about the tremendous benefits of social responsibility for children. Apart from making a difference in their community, there are some personal merits for this. Great skills are developed through volunteer experiences that go beyond doing good work. We were astounded by our children's access to professional training while volunteering at a hospital. They would never have been hired for the jobs, but their position as volunteers allowed them to gain experience at a young age.

Encourage their interests. Forget those clichés about what is of interest to teenagers. There are a lot of things that they are interested in, and those interests can inspire them to engage in activities beyond what they would normally do. Provide opportunities for them to turn their hobbies into moments of social responsibility. The child who is into making hip-hop beats might be encouraged to create a song that will teach children the alphabet, days of the week, or the elements of the periodic table.

Pair their interests with community activities. Using your teen's interests, look up local community events, causes or activities that are aligned with those interests. Teens who are nurturers would be happy volunteering in hospitals. Those who love animals would feel fulfilled working in an animal shelter. Teens with no visible interests may learn about their community through a local rally.

Be an example. This is a recurrent theme throughout this book, and it has played out in every chapter. If you want your children to be more involved in things that that are of interest to you, then you should be involved in those activities. Modeling for your teen will do more than anything that you will say.

Supporting

On an intellectual level, you already know the difference between parenting and policing. But knowing it is one thing, and then clearly respecting that line in practical terms is another story. At a younger age, your children may have come to you if they needed anything. You have raised them to be self-reliant and independent. Now is the time to allow them to exert their independence.

The teenage years are when you may need to understand that the child who was so dependent on you, is doing things for themselves. They are also doing things that do not involve you. This can be disorienting. Some children take on a part-time paid job or sign up for internship programs beyond school. This does not automatically mean independence, but you may start to notice that they are making decisions without you. This seemingly abrupt cutting-off can make you seem less in control. Avoid trying to exert control like restricting their movements. Instead, embrace their independence as a way of them becoming their own person. Get used to witnessing their mistakes and support them as they think through and solve their own problems. Resist the urge to solve their problems even if their problem involves another adult.

Think less about control and more about a shift in the relationship. The family values that have been established will serve as your teen's touch point. Empower your teen by allowing them to make their own decisions and demanding that they embrace the consequence. Try to avoid only relying on the way that you were reared. Those things that worked or didn't work for you may be different for your child. Always allow your relationship with your child to be unique. You will be informed by the way that you were parented. Take those strategies that helped you grow and embrace them but also try other techniques that may be new to you.

Every waking day in the life of your teen should be about choices. Teens are not like adults who are self-assured and more structured, and therefore know what to expect most days. Adults are more in control of their choices. The teen, on the other hand, is being pulled in multiple directions when it comes to making choices. Do not try to make choices for them. Allow them to go through the process and learn from their choices.

There are so many areas of concern where their choices could impact their future. Areas like sex, faith, the kind of friends they keep, their extra-curricular activities and education choices will affect who they are as an adult. As a parent, your job is not to control any of those choices but to serve as their guide. It is more important for you to be one of the individuals in their lives from whom they can seek counsel than the counsel that you actually give.

It will help if you are truthful about things. For instance, on the issue of sex, you have to be honest. Try to stay away from gender or religious-based conversations. The experiences of both genders are different, but the outcome when it comes to choices are the same. Using religious doctrine to control your child's behavior rarely works in the long run. Use relatable experiences to reinforce the message you want to convey to them. Be okay if they decide for themselves to do something different from what you expect them to do. If you have experiences relating to what they are going through, share with them, and when you share with them, try not to share just your triumphs. Tell them of your failures too. When teenagers see bits and pieces of themselves in you, they will be more open to your guidance in helping them make the right decisions.

You started the process of helping your child set goals for themselves. Your teen will feel pressure from society to articulate future plans. Reinforce the fact that goal setting is a lifelong skill that serves as an active motivator in those things you are trying to achieve. It helps your teen see the possibility of achieving their dreams when they set realistic measurable goals and achieve them through deliberate action. Goal setting should not be limited to grand projects like where they want to be in a decade. Children should start with something as simple as using their Spanish language skills to converse with the serving staff at a Mexican restaurant. The objective is to encourage your teen to set goals and track when they have achieved those goals.

To set a goal, your teen would have to look inwards and find out what they really want to achieve. They should then draft a step-by-step plan that would help them achieve those goals. After setting those goals, your teen should use their plan to work towards achieving the goal. To maximize the impact, the goals and outcomes should always be written. Individuals who develop the habit of writing goals and revisiting them to see if they have been met tend to be more successful. This process helps your teen identify what they want, and the experiences they learn on the journey to achieving their goals will help sharpen their self-efficacy skills.

In the process of achieving their goals at this stage, you may need to provide additional support. For instance, if your teen wants to improve their performance in sports, they will need to attend practice and even work on essential skills after practice. If they are interested in honing their skill, you might hire someone to help them develop it. Be prepared to play a supportive role in assisting them to achieve their goals. Sometimes, that role is active, and other times it is passive. So, be supportive, whether you are driving them to their activity or simply cheering from the sidelines.

Finally, when your teen achieves their goal, allow them a moment to enjoy their victory, but don't let it end there. Encourage them to set new goals that challenge them. When this becomes a habit for them, you can be assured your teen will grow into a high-achieving adult who is pragmatic, confident, and has a good sense of what they want.

Growth Opportunities

There are so many great opportunities for teens to engage in beyond their physical environment or the community where they live. Many of these opportunities may not have been available to you, or you may not have been aware of them. Encourage your teen to research and participate in these opportunities when they are introduced to them.

A gap year is typically the period of time that a high school student might take prior to transitioning. During that year, young people actively engage in all types of experiences. Thank you, Malia Obama, for popularizing this amazing opportunity that all young people should consider. Many people think of a gap year experience between high school and college. A gap year can also be a year between when your teen transitions from your home to another activity. This can also be a period of time before going into the military or the world of work. There are opportunities that should be considered between college and entering the workforce or enrolling in graduate school. Opportunities such as the Peace Corps and City Year are great gap year experiences right after an undergraduate experience.

There were people in our environments who saw the success that our children were experiencing as young adults and asked if we would work with their children. We would invite them to spend the summer with us some time while they were in high school.

While the students stayed with us and researched opportunities, they were completely self-sufficient. They were responsible for preparing their own food except on the days when George was sneaking them out of the house for a special lunch or dinner. There were even lessons in these excursions as the young people were taken to upscale restaurants where they typically would not go. Subtle lessons in decorum and polite conversations were achieved through modeling. This exercise to improve social-emotional development is simple, but it is invaluable for developing adolescents' sense of self as they explore experiences outside of their comfort zone.

During this experience, students were directed to research various opportunities. Individuals enrolled in culinary workshops and set up a college tour at higher education institutions within walking distance from our home. Through conversations, we coached them in the process of finding the information, and then they contacted representatives in the organizations. They managed their time in setting up the appointments and tours. They figured out how to negotiate the neighborhood to get to where they were going. At times this included figuring out the city mass transit system, and at other times it meant figuring out how to walk to their destination.

During these excursions, there can be moments of confusion where signs are unclear, or the young person is not as used to engaging in unknown activities. Walking students through problem-solving when they run into challenges prepares them more for the world than simply providing them with the answer. These activities purposefully put them in situations where they had to solve problems.

We can never forget the lesson that is to be learned in failure. There are times when we believe that a student failing an assignment, an exam, or even a course would spell doom. Parents, guardians, and adults who are responsible for the rearing of young children need to allow them to fail. It is important not to focus on the failure but on the lesson that can be learned. There is the ever-important lesson of perseverance. When one fails at something, the test of character is when they try again and even fail multiple times again. We often focus so much on the outcome that we forget all the lessons in going through the process.

Failure also offers lessons to humility. If young people miss an appointment, or in some other way inconvenience someone, it is important to help them make the necessary amends. Many times this is in the form of a formal message of apology. This causes the young person to acknowledge the impact their actions may have had on another person and then to offer an apology.

You can always start the process of having young people engage in varied activities by not discrediting their dreams. In this stage, they may have a sense of what they want to do and who they want to be but may not be articulate enough to phrase it in a way that captures its real essence. A family friend told us of how their daughter, at age six, told them that she wanted to sell corn when she grew up because of her love for sweet corn. For her parents, who were very accomplished in their respective careers, it was not the kind of dream they wanted for their little girl, who expected not only to go to college but to be admitted to an Ivy League institution. Thankfully, they didn't toss her dream aside. Today, their daughter manages a chain of restaurants across the country, and of course their menu features sweet corn.

Believe in their dream. This part is vital if you are going to promote their ambitions and nurture their dreams. Believing in their dreams reinforces their confidence and puts you in a better position to see a pathway to achieving their dreams. This brings us to the next point: To prevent burnout, or worse, your child's loss of faith in their dreams, you need to help them celebrate every step they take on this journey. Some dreams take a while to achieve, and in that time, a lot of things will happen. Encouraging them to have tiny celebrations reminds them that they are on track as each step brings them closer to their dreams.

Acceptance is the first step in supporting your teen's ambitions. You have to embrace your child for who they are. Some of their strengths and talents may not match with your personal vision for them, but you must train yourself to understand that your child has their own desires and ambitions. Open yourself up and accept them for who they are.

Be observant. In an earlier chapter, we warned you against the dangers of signing your child up for everything that you saw other parents sign their children up for because you confused pictures on the wall in cute dance outfits with good parenting. Ask your child about their interests and then provide the resource for extra classes or sourcing materials to help them perfect what they can do effortlessly.

Resist the urge to go all in at this stage. Children in this age group are still evolving. While you are encouraging their passions, grooming their talents, and nurturing their strengths, you should look at this stage as merely assessing if your child would like to take things further.

Remove the pressure of your expectation. This is not to say you should not have expectations entirely because that would only deliver the opposite result. What we are saying is that you should set a cap on your expectations. For now, instead of expecting your youngster to become the best at what they do, encourage them to give it their best. An A is great, but the focus should be on the process as opposed to the result. You should assess whether they are working hard enough, whether they are struggling, and whether they are happy.

Maintain a balance. Academically, there are certain subjects that schools may insist are mandatory regardless of your child's interests or strengths. This applies to life in general as well. Expose them to areas they may not be strong in and encourage them to at least try the experience. This may never translate into excellent performance from the child in that area, but at the very least, it gives them foundational knowledge that is never wasted.

For most part of this stage, your teen should be encouraged to spend their time trying to discover who they are. They will try out new hairstyles, fashion, and music. This immersion into self can make them seem oblivious to the rest of the world and even members of their family. It makes it difficult to remain loving and nurturing all the time towards them. What is important to remember is not the behavior, but the fact that your teen is a human being going through a phase where they are trying to find themselves. If you have provided a good foundation, you should not worry about your teens' change in moods, attitudes and behaviors. Even if you do not feel as if a proper foundation has been provided, you should resist the urge to influence your teens' decisions. Have an open mind and trust that you have provided them with the necessities they will require as you attempt to give balanced parenting. Even as they make mistakes, with your love and support, they will have the capacity to rebound and continue to thrive.

"The children who need love the most
would ask for it in the most unloving ways."

-Russel Barkley

A THOUSAND YEARS OF SOLITUDE: AGES 19 – 25

"We worry about what the child would become tomorrow
Yet we forget that he is someone today."

Stacia Tauscher

PREMISES

The emerging adulthood years are marked by a bit of the experimentation and exploration of the adolescence stage as individuals in this stage try to figure out what career paths to take, what their dressing identity will be, what lifestyle they want to adopt, or what partners they want to be with, among others. This explains why the stage is considered a transition phase between adolescence and full-fledged adulthood. If well lived, the years of emerging adulthood can serve to resolve any pending identity issues from adolescence and to enter adulthood with greater developmental stability.

The rapid physical changes of the previous developmental stages greatly slow down after adolescence. What has been achieved in earlier stages of development now "begins to perform" in the emerging adulthood stage. During emerging adulthood, the peak of physiological development will show in muscle strength, refined sensory abilities, maximum brain function, optimal cardiac and lung function, and reproductive capacities. Motor skills are operating at their best, and emerging adults in physical sports professions will put forth their best performances. A considerable number of women have their first child during this time.

An individual's capacity for independent decision-making is particularly related to the emergence of adulthood. This is majorly dependent on an emerging adult's cognitive skills, especially the ability to weigh options before making decisions. Unlike adolescents who think abstractly and can be idealistic, emerging adults will consider the possible outcome in a situation and the likely outcome, making their thinking more practical and realistic. This is linked to wider experience and the realization that expectations and possibilities do not always become a reality.

Cognitive skills in emerging adults are also characterized by flexible thinking. This is especially seen in the individual's capacity to consider opposing viewpoints and positions. It is considered a core marker in post formal thinking because it is more realistic that few realities and viewpoints are either completely right or completely wrong. This would explain why an emerging adult who thought his/her parents were complete angels or devils will now see them as persons with strengths and weaknesses like every normal person.

Cognitive development in emerging adulthood is also characterized by the individual's capacity to be more balanced and flexible in their thinking, independent of what others think, delay gratification and ignore unnecessary input, and factor in contextual elements when cognitively evaluating situations.

The years after adolescence are a tricky transition in the relationship between parents and their emerging adults. More than a parent-child relationship, the two are now adults, and parents can find it difficult to accept this fact and let the emerging adult in their son or daughter find their own identity. Parents can hinder identity formation among emerging adults, especially if the young adults are still living with their parents. Instead, leaving home promotes independence and identity development.

Most emerging adults will not consider themselves ready for lasting intimate relationship commitments until they are in their late twenties or early thirties, but they may be into strong friendships and important acquaintances. Those who have not successfully negotiated their identity by this time are more likely to fall into social isolation.

A key developmental element during these years is also defined by the educational options that emerging adults commit to. College years help in defining one's identity and career preferences while at the same time opening them up to diverse political, cultural, and ethnic realities and ideas. This helps them build a more complex self-concept, more stable self-esteem, and a clear awareness of their changing values and characteristics.

Language development in emerging adulthood is influenced by various factors that are proper to this stage. First, pursuing higher education increasingly exposes emerging adults to language in its multiple variants, including learning a second or third language. This widens their scope of knowledge, content comprehension, and interaction with diverse cultures. However, this can also limit the usage and proficiency of their first language for those who have to use it less.

Emerging adults may also manifest phonetic variations due to changes in the social context. This may come as a result of regional or international mobility and manifest in significant changes of accent. New work environments can also contribute to language developmental changes if emerging adults allow this to happen.

Individuals in the emerging adulthood phase manifest higher articulation rates in speech and reading when compared to children, adolescents, and older adults. This is explained by the fact that brain development in emerging adults is at its peak, and most of the individuals in this developmental phase are majorly college students who are engaged in extensive reading on a regular basis.

Building a moral identity is part of the overall identity development in emerging adulthood. In this developmental stage, emerging adults have the task of developing a clear sense of morality and moral values, which are key in defining their moral identity. Most individuals struggle with developing a moral identity that directs their daily behavior; instead, they tend to make moral decisions with little self-reflection. Nonetheless, the responsibilities of life characteristic of emerging adulthood promote advanced levels of moral reasoning.

As with identity formation, emerging adults may still be working on defining their moral identity. Beyond struggling with what constitutes good or bad behavior, individuals work to establish a sense of morality and a direction for their life.

Once mature moral development has been achieved, emerging adults can go beyond socially accepted values to adopt a more inclusive approach. They now understand that different societies have different value systems and that certain values (life, freedom, justice, etc.) and human rights are universal and should be placed above single cultures because they are prerequisites for a good society.

This realization explains why emerging adults and adults in later stages go against their society to stand for universal values that transcend those of their single societies. Even though they are not in favor of breaking laws, they know the values of an ideal society must be protected.

It is during this stage that many people experience true independence. However, emerging adults are not completely independent as, in many ways, they are still dependent on parents for support, such as finances. In many other ways, their lives are expanding. They are legally recognized as having attained the age of consent. They gain a voice politically as they now have the right to vote. This extends into their social lives as well. Bars, clubs and events that were usually age-restricted now become accessible.

One of the most significant defining qualities of being an adult is the ability to make firm decisions for themselves. For a parent of an emerging adult, their defining quality would be the ability to accept the decisions their child has made, whether they support it or not. During this stage, it is expected that the opinions of the emerging adult on most issues are fully formulated.

PERSPECTIVES

Transitions - George

Curtis' journey from high school to college, to the business world, and finally to graduate school was fascinating. Curtis started our expectation of international engagement by identifying an opportunity to study for the summer in Costa Rica. He participated in a study abroad program between the summer of his junior and senior years in high school. This was certainly surprising to us because while he was in high school, Curtis did not embrace academic activities. He was a tremendous high school athlete, and starting his sophomore year in high school, he was highly recruited by some of the most prestigious football programs in the United States. He spent most of his summers at football camps.

After graduating from high school, he attended Virginia Tech on a full athletic scholarship. The summer after his freshman year, he developed rhabdomyolysis—a condition that occurs when damaged muscle tissue releases its proteins and electrolytes into the blood—after a particularly grueling workout. This serious medical condition could have been fatal or resulted in permanent disability. Muscles in his heart, back, and legs were damaged, and his kidneys failed. After spending significant time in the hospital and a year rehabilitating, Curtis made the decision to return to college. Coach Frank Beamer committed to honoring his athletic scholarship at Virginia Tech until he finished his degree, but refused to allow him to be on the team.

Curtis informed me that he was transferring to Morgan State University because it had his major, and he would be allowed to continue his collegiate football career. We explained to him that we had saved money in anticipation of him going to college, and there was no need to play football anymore. We were very concerned for his health. For his entire life, I always insisted that whatever he started, he would bring to its logical conclusion. However, for me putting his health in jeopardy was a logical conclusion. He told me that, in no uncertain terms, he had to finish what he started because it was in his head. He insisted that if he did not complete his collegiate football career, he would regret it for the rest of his life. This was one of the saddest days of my life because I was afraid my son would die if he continued to play football following his recent health scare.

We were fortunate that he completed his football career, earning honors as an all Mid-Eastern Athletic Conference (MEAC) tackle and completing his bachelor of science degree in urban planning and architectural design. Although he was a very successful football player, I think he was only a fraction of himself at the end of his football career. However, at 50%, Curtis could take on and beat most players he ran into who were at 100%. He was very good at what he did. Once football was out of his system, he transitioned to the next phase of his life.

Engaging With Other Adults – Tina

As teenagers, we always insisted that the children engage with adults in their lives (i.e., family members, teachers, coaches, advisors). Many of these individuals had views that were very different from ours. We always encouraged Curtis and Nia to seek counsel and then make their own decisions.

Curtis called me from college because he ran into a situation and wanted my advice. He was told by the chairperson of his department that he could not play football and keep his major in architectural and environmental design. I explained that I thought the chair meant that it would be difficult to keep up with the work and be an athlete. Curtis assured me that the chair emphatically told him he would need to quit football or change his major.

I then asked if this was a policy that was written in a catalog, to which he said no while rolling his eyes. I can only imagine. I asked if he had been consulting his course syllabi for due dates and spoke to all his professors about whether they wanted work turned in early if he would miss classes because he was on travel with the team. He assured me that he would continue this practice since this was something he had been doing even in high school. So, I suggested that he ignore the chair and continue what he was doing. I told him that faculty members were present to provide counsel, but he was not obligated to take it. He completed his football career and his academic program.

Nia had a similar situation with an academic advisor. During her freshman year, she decided to engage in a study abroad program. She found a program, applied, and was accepted. As a part of the administrative process, she had to have the signature of her academic advisor. Her advisor told her that it wasn't a good idea, and he refused to sign the paperwork.

Nia called me about the situation. I explained to her that her advisor was approaching this situation from the perspective that studying abroad could possibly get in the way of her completing her program of study. The engineering field has a high attrition rate, and activities like studying abroad typically cause students to graduate later than intended. Many college students believe that they are successful if they graduate in four years. I asked her if that mattered to her. She said it didn't, so I suggested that she go to another administrator to get the signature. She completed the study abroad and graduated with an engineering degree.

The Greatest Gift to Humanity – George

One of our favorite family stories is about Nia's graduation speech after completing her baccalaureate degree from Howard University. At the party in her honor, she was really excited about thanking her family and friends during the obligatory graduation speech. She told the family that when she ran into difficulties, she would call her mother first, and her mother would give her a long lecture on the subject. Then she called me, and I told her to "be the Nia."

During that speech, she announced that she would not be taking any of the lucrative professional positions she had been offered. She would not be enrolling in any competitive graduate programs to which she was admitted. She announced to the family that she was going to accept a post working in Benin through the Peace Corps. Numerous family members would approach her to tell her what a bad idea this was.

On one hand, Curtis was highly recruited in athletics, but Nia was highly recruited in academics. She had several scholarship offers from different institutions. She had many things going for her, but what really made her stand out was her tenacity and willingness to follow the road less traveled.

When Nia was in high school, she participated in an exchange program through Rotary International. She spent the 11th grade in Brazil. Along with learning to live with other families and learning new cultures, she mastered Portuguese and completed all her schoolwork using her new language. She went on to attend Howard University, where she majored in computer engineering. During her sophomore year, she went to Japan and studied at Chubu University, taking engineering, culture, and language courses. Again, she embraced living with a Japanese family and learning a new culture while mastering the Japanese language.

After completing her undergraduate degree, she applied to several graduate programs, interviewed with various companies, and applied for the Peace Corps. She was admitted to a couple of graduate programs and offered positions where she would make a six-figure income. She was also accepted into the Peace Corps program.

I remember her asking me about possibly attending the Peace Corps after graduation. My answer to her was straightforward. I paraphrased a Bible verse and told her that to whom much is given, much is required. I reminded her of the many opportunities that she was given, and the fact that she took advantage of those opportunities was a good thing. I also reminded her that when opportunities come her way in life, she should have the emotional fortitude to take advantage of them. I reminded her that she needed to remember to give back. She made a choice to accept the Peace Corps offer and to spend two and a half years in Benin. It was while she was living and working in Benin that she mastered her third language, French. She indeed continued to "be the Nia."

Making His Way – George

Curtis is the type of person who typically stays in one place when he settles on an activity. Once he completed his undergraduate degree, he did not have a position in his field. I don't think architecture or urban planning was a part of his passion. I think he went into the field because he thought that was something he might want to pursue when he studied it and gained some interest.

During his senior year in college, he volunteered at a transition home for troubled youth. After graduation, he was offered a permanent job at the home, and they really loved him. We were certain that after spending time working in this position that he would want to pursue the field of social work. As his parents, we were totally against this. I thought it was a bad idea because Curt was a big man, and I knew he had a great appetite. In my opinion, he needed to make some money, and we didn't feel that profession would afford him the kind of life he would want to live.

Service was always a part of both children's orientation. However, I knew Curt would naturally find a way of serving humanity regardless of his profession. He went into project management and construction, and his background in architecture was a perfect match for him. He started out with a small firm on the college campus where I worked. While living in Columbia, he would play basketball at the local YMCA. He was such a personable young man that he caught the attention of an executive from a large company out of Columbia. The executive gave him a position as a project manager.

Curtis became successful in his position but wanted to pursue further study. We talked about some of the programs that he was interested in. There was a graduate program in project management at Clemson, and there was a master's program in transportation at South Carolina State University. He asked me what I thought about the programs. I told him that I did not see the logic behind getting a master's degree in an area that he had already mastered.

I told him that transportation was the future, and it was an area related to planning and project management, but that it would expand his expertise. Curtis enrolled in the transportation program at SCSU. Not only was this my alma mater, but Tina and I worked at the university when Curtis was younger. Throughout his entire time as a graduate student at SCSU, he never mentioned to anyone his relationship to us, even though it would have helped him. Even when he ran into trouble, he always talked with Tina or I about the situation, but never asked me to intercede on his behalf. And I never did.

We were really surprised by his work in his graduate program because he never showed an interest in academics. We always knew that Curtis was very intelligent, but I thought that his strength was in writing. He never put a lot of effort into academics. Many of his professors noticed that he had exceptional analytical skills and was an excellent student. At the end of his master's, one of his professors took a position at the University of Massachusetts in Lowell and invited Curtis to join him to work on his doctorate. Curtis earned a doctorate in civil engineering with a concentration in transportation.

Go Where People Want You – George

Nia found herself at a crossroads after graduating from Howard University with a bachelor's degree in computer engineering and a minor in Japanese. She spent two and a half years in the Peace Corps. She wanted to continue her formal studies. While in Benin, she applied to several computer engineering graduate programs. Nia was interested in programs at Auburn University and Columbia University. Nia has always wanted to live in New York, and there was a professor at Columbia who was doing research that she was interested in. Columbia was only giving her partial funding, and Auburn was giving her full funding.

As a father, I was very upset that Columbia didn't see Nia's brilliance and the potential of this young woman. I knew that Columbia was an institution that had plenty of talented people. I always wanted my daughter to understand if people don't want you, you don't need to go that way. This is especially true when you're in an academic environment. I encouraged her to go where they were going to provide her with the most funding.

I believe there are times that you are at a disadvantage in a program when you are competing against other people that the institution believes in because they provided them with full funding. The institution is going to work very hard to ensure that they are successful because that is where the institution invested its resources. In an already competitive environment, I wanted Nia to know that she would need all the support she could get and that she should go to an institution where she was their top pick.

I really thought that Nia would regret the decision if she decided to enroll in the program in Columbia. I knew that so many social factors were pulling her towards the city's bright lights. In a last-ditch effort to drive my point home, I bought a car and told her that the keys to the car would be in Auburn, Alabama. Nia attended graduate school at Auburn University.

Although Nia's intent was to complete the master's and doctorate at Auburn, things did not go that way. When things did not work out, she completed the master's program and applied to other doctoral programs. She was provided with full funding by several programs. She was leaning toward the electrical and computer engineering program at Northwestern University because she felt it would be more comfortable for her. She was always concerned that her technical skills would not allow her to compete in a program that was consistently recognized for their work in machine learning and speech processing.

When we asked her about her interview with Carnegie Mellon University, she said the focus of their conversation was on the fact that she spoke three languages beyond English (Portuguese, Japanese, and French) and that she was an American citizen. She had the unique qualities of having two degrees in computer engineering and a working knowledge of four languages. This made her a unique member of their research team, and they were more than happy to have her and to provide her with full funding.

Although Nia struggled in her doctoral program, she earned an electrical and computer engineering doctorate focused on natural language processing. She had really great professors. I thought they were people who pushed her and made her go beyond what she thought she could do. Tina and I would have dinner with Bhikasha Raj, her faculty mentor, and talk about how we, too, had battled to help Nia realize how talented she was. We all agreed that Nia has one thing going for her that most naturally talented people don't have. Nia has always been extremely hard-working. She has grit and a great work ethic. In my opinion, that is what makes her an excellent mother, an excellent wife, and an excellent professional. If Nia sets her eyes on something she's passionate about, she rarely misses the target.

PROMISES

One very important thing we have learned as parents over the years is that children grow every day regardless of their age. Watching young people develop distinct personalities and finding their own way into the world is filled with emotion. You will be delighted to discover what they will become and what they will accomplish while also feeling sadness, fear, and yearning.

Communication is never more important than in this phase. The way that you speak with emerging adults will shape your relationship and theirs as well. It is more important than ever to get to know them and to support them as they continue to grow and develop. Keep the lines of communication open and resist judging their decisions. Work on keeping an open mind and practice active listening.

Although it is difficult, advice should be given only when asked for. Even in instances where you believe that the emerging adult's decisions will have serious implications for the rest of their life. It is important to remember that it is their life, and the final decision is theirs. Remember that modeling appropriate behavior or good decision-making is never too late. Emerging adults also appreciate and can use heavy doses of honesty. Don't be afraid to share stories of when you made bad decisions and how you feel about the outcomes. They will feel empowered that you are treating them with respect given to adults. They will also appreciate seeing the adults in their life as humans who make mistakes just like they do.

Regardless of what has occurred in the past, give your emerging adults a clean slate. Forget about past missteps and look forward to their continued growth and development. For the most part, you just need to focus on who they are now.

Show genuine interest in what they do. The world evolves constantly, and the emerging adult in your life may engage in completely foreign activities. Take every opportunity to learn from them and to understand what excites them. Ask questions that indicate that you really want to know about what they are doing. Give them gifts that support their activities. Talk to others in their presence about what they are doing so that they know you are proud of them.

Your emerging adult is not always going to make decisions that you approve of. It may be hard to stand by knowing that this young person's choices may not be the best thing for them. It is not right to coerce or force them to do things differently. Even if it hurts you, you should maintain your boundaries. As a parent, you cannot simply walk away. It is your obligation as a parent to advise and assist your children.

When your child is an emerging adult, it may be difficult to remember that this is the time for them to make their own decisions and to suffer the consequences of their decisions. Although this process should have started a lot earlier in their lives, some of the decisions they make as emerging adults will impact their entire lives. Some of these decisions may include altering their bodies, getting married, or having children. Regardless of how you feel about any of these decisions, the decisions are theirs to make.

Be supportive. In certain scenarios, you would rather bite your tongue than hold their hands through this decision. But if your goal is to maintain a healthy relationship with your emerging adult, you and your feelings are going to have to take a backseat. If they ask you about a particular decision, offer your response in a way that is respectful and recognize that the final decision is theirs. Suggest that they consult with other people in their lives that they respect. When all is done, and your emerging adult makes the decision, the next best thing is to be supportive.

Counsel your emerging adult from a place of love. Contain your emotions as much as possible and speak from a place free of judgment. Whether this is a decision that has been taken or is yet to be taken, have an open and honest conversation with your emerging adult only if they are asking you to be a part of the decision. For instance, if your emerging adult has decided to get married, but both she and her fiancé are still full-time students who would like to live in your home, you have the right to discuss the part of their decision involving them moving into your home. You have every right and should refuse their request to live with you, but that should not be mixed with their decision to get married.

If your emerging adult asks to return home for any reason, you should decide with clear ideas about what the situation is going to look like with as much detail as possible. If the decision is that the young adult will pay rent, then the amount, terms and conditions should be in writing. Once you have decided to allow your emerging adult to move back into your home, be okay with the decision.

Above all, commit to keeping the lines of communication open so that if anyone starts feeling uncomfortable, they will speak to others in the living arrangement as soon as possible. This may be uncomfortable, but it could save your relationship over the course of your lives. Careful attention should be paid to ensure that all parties are communicating effectively before, during, and after decisions are made. Never be afraid of involving a neutral party, such as a professional counselor. Avoid bringing in other family members or friends if conflicts arise.

Don't take responsibility for the actions of your emerging adult. Even if you did not do everything you could to help your emerging adult in the early phases of their lives, keep in mind that you are just human. If wishes were horses, beggars would ride on them. Therefore, you can't go back in time and redo actions. If your actions were terrible, forgive yourself, ask your emerging adult for forgiveness and make corrective actions moving forward. Overcompensating for past mistakes only makes matters worse.

You reared them to be who they are. And like all humans, they will still make mistakes. Speak openly and honestly about decisions that you made in rearing them and your thoughts at the time. Try to be as open and honest about the mistakes that you feel that you made when you were their age. Talk about lessons learned and how those lessons have impacted your life. Consistently let them know that you love and respect them and that you will always be there to support them.

Get along with the people in their lives. Your emerging adult's circle will consist of friends, business partners, in-laws and perhaps a significant other. Whatever your feelings are about these individuals, particularly their significant other, keep your relationship with them civil and respectful. Keep your feelings to yourself. Remember that if your emerging adult can sleep with them, you can sit with them.

There is a difference between staying engaged and smothering. The primary difference is that the decision is a shared experience. What is going on in their lives may determine how engaged they want to be with you. Whether they are living on their own, or with you until they can get on their feet, their lives are their own as adults. They have the right to make decisions about who they want in their lives and to what extent. It will be helpful for you to manage your expectations of how your emerging adult will engage with you.

For your emerging adult, you want them to win, you want them to thrive, and you want them to do it on their own terms. This is what the journey is about, and it is only when you let go that you can really see all that they have accomplished and what they have the potential to be.

"Education begins the moment we see our children as innately wise and capable beings.
Only then can we play along in their world."

Vincent Corain

ALL QUIET ON THE WESTERN FRONT: AGES 26 AND ABOVE

"Seven things every child needs to hear:
I love you
I am proud of you
I'm sorry
I forgive you
I'm listening
This is your responsibility
You have what it takes to succeed"

Sherrie Campbell

PREMISES

By this stage, your children have entered adulthood. The postformal thinking of emerging adulthood continues to characterize the adulthood years. As young adults, your children are better at using the problem-solving that is built on deep reflection on life situations and realities.

In early adulthood, individuals manifest complex postformal thought by considering multiple aspects of a problem or situation. They can contextualize issues and are aware that a problem in one context may not have a similar solution in a different context. They can also perceive the underlying complexities in a situation and factor them into their decision-making.

Individuals in early adulthood will also manifest higher levels of wisdom, which is the expert knowledge about the practical aspects of life, which helps in excellent judgment about important matters and the understanding of how to cope with difficult life situations. Research has, however, suggested that few people only acquire high levels of wisdom and that the period of late adolescence and early adulthood are the stages of attaining wisdom. When it comes to information processing, early adulthood individuals have greater information processing speeds than older adults because they have more fluid intelligence. This means that they have a greater capacity to learn new things and skills faster and abstractly.

Socioemotional development in young adulthood is about your children's ability to integrate emotional experiences into significant and pleasant social relationships. In the first years of early adulthood, most young adults make a permanent commitment to an intimate partner. Romantic relationships prior to and during marriage in early adulthood individuals may reproduce childhood attachment patterns. Those patterns will be secure, avoidant, or resistant, impacting their relationship with their significant other. Early adulthood individuals are still negotiating the intimacy versus isolation crisis. Your children may still be trying to embrace their independence and feel pressure to be in a committed relationship.

As with other domains of human development, moral development would be expected to peak in adulthood. That would mean your adult children will chronologically proceed to the highest stage of moral development, which has been described as the morality of universal ethical principles. In other words, your children will understand the difference between right and wrong and should act in ways that are correct.

It is possible that your young adult child may still judge moral situations based on the "good boy/good girl" morality characteristic of the early years of adolescence. Or they may consider the law and social order morality, which is characteristic of late adolescence and which is thought to be the level where most adults remain. From this approach, moral development for most adults is built around maintaining the proper behavior of a loyal citizen and dutifully obeying laws. The moral development stage at which an adult will remain may be determined by factors such as family upbringing, cognitive changes, emotions, peers, culture, and neurodevelopment.

The few adults who attain a higher level of moral development judge moral situations based on universal ethical principles of justice and the preservation of life regardless of the laws of specific societies. Your child may go against specific social laws and rules if they do not conform to higher moral principles that promote justice and defend the lives of all. This may be in conflict with your own morals. For this group, defending what is universally right by the principle of justice is more important than being loyal citizens.

PERSPECTIVES

Our Gifts to the World – George & Tina

At this time, Curtis and Nia are adults. They brought two beautiful children into our lives: Tyachenna and Jason. We have five beautiful grandchildren: Isaiah, Alyssah, Sydney, Elijah and Elle. We couldn't be prouder of the adults that Curtis and Nia have become. By society's standards, they are successful citizens. By our standards, they are great human beings.

Our intention as parents was to raise individuals who would benefit the world. We wanted them to see themselves as a part of the human family. We had the luxury of being able to be deliberate and intentional about the decisions we made in their upbringing. There were times that we exerted pressure, and then there were times when we felt that life was the better teacher. The results speak for themselves, and we look forward to engaging as their parents as they make their way through the next phase of their lives.

PROMISES

The phrase by Sherrie Campbell struck a chord with us as we were carrying out research for this book. While we use this in the book's final chapter, it is meant to be a regular feature throughout every stage of your child's life. The words you speak to your child continue to impact them even though they are adults. At this point, where they have fully established their own life, these words will support their confidence, making them believe that they can overcome their weaknesses and lay the foundation for the next generation.

The primary reason we reserved the introductory quote for the last chapter is that at this stage, there really isn't so much you can give that would be appreciated as much as words of encouragement. You have been with your children throughout the entire process. You have witnessed their vulnerable moments, and you have seen them show extreme courage as well. Your experiences may differ, but you understand where they come from.

Even if you don't work in the same field as your child, they may come to you with career-related problems hoping you can provide insight. There will always be something that they might call you up for. If you have a good relationship with them, this makes it easier for them. No one knows them as much as you do, and this gives you insight into their personality that not many would have. Even their spouses would need to spend years with them before figuring this out. With all this information, it is easy to cross lines and offer unsolicited advice. Remember to practice active listening and reserve your opinions for when they are requested.

There has been a lot of talk about children feeling entitled to their parents' wealth but not many people talk about parents feeling entitled to the wealth of their children. Parents may have sacrificed a lot for their children during the years that they were their primary caregivers. This is not to say that children should not consider caring for their parents when they need it. However, it may not always be convenient. This may be the case when the child has a family of their own to care for.

In some cultures, the primary family consists of the parents and their children, whereas in many cultures the primary family includes extended family members. The nature of these relationships is heavily dependent on the way that the child was reared. If you care for elders in the extended family in a close intimate way, it increases the probability that this is the way that your child will interact and care for you. However, if they observed that you treated the elders in the family as burdens, then this may be how your children have learned that extended family members should be treated.

If you have not made plans for life after rearing children, it is never too early to start thinking about what you will do with your time. A good transition plan improves your quality of life when you get older and increases the probability that you will be satisfied during this period in your life. Whether you live far away from your children or close by, in times of crisis, they will always be there for you. Having your finances in order would make it that much easier for them to be there for you.

When you start your own family, you create family traditions guided by your values. You may notice some differences if you compare your family traditions with those of your parents. There will be a repeat of this pattern with your children. In some ways, they may honor some of the traditions they grew up with, but you can expect that there will be other traditions and practices that they adopt as their own.

The reasons for those changes could depend on several factors. But the most likely one is probably based on the person they bring into your life. Your children's partners will have their own ideas and traditions to bring to the relationship. In a healthy relationship, there will be a blending of these ideas and activities.

Family traditions are birthed from the merging of values. Although you and your child may have some shared values, there are areas where compromises must be made. Those areas of compromise will determine family traditions. It is not always easy to manage an extended family that may include two sets of grandparents and a host of extended family members. This is often a source of tension when it is time to visit and spend time with family. Since most holidays are about family, your children might be conflicted over who and where to spend the holidays with. The best way to address these tensions is to create new holiday traditions.

In our family, as we all got married, there was a struggle to figure out when we would visit family during major holiday seasons. We came from very large close families. We appreciated that G-G-Pop, Tina's father, claimed the Memorial Day Weekend as the time that he wanted all of his children to gather at his home. There were rarely any conflicts as this was not a popular holiday season. Over the years, this has become one of the most significant family get-togethers for us.

You should also know that your children are not the only ones creating new family traditions at this point. You and your partner may have to come up with traditions of your own. Now that the nest is empty, certain things you did together as a family may not be the same without them. There are some things you would do out of habit, but you would always feel the absence of the children. Instead of focusing on the emptiness, look at this as a time to start setting new goals and creating new traditions for yourselves. It may be a little intimidating initially, but we all know that life's great adventures start the same way.

Once upon a time, you were one of the most powerful influences in your children's lives. Certain decisions could not be made without your consent. Your adult child is now making all these life-altering decisions without even informing you about them. There may even be a time when they are making decisions about you. It is important to remain flexible and open-minded regarding your relationship with your adult children.

Your adult children may consult with you every now and then on issues that require external input from someone they trust, but ultimately, they will make their own choices. A lot of parents struggle with this. They go the extra mile to exert themselves and their opinions in these situations. This is the ultimate form of disrespect for an adult child because that parent completely disregards their person.

You have to accept that your child is an adult capable of making their own decisions. By making their own decisions, they are not disrespecting you. They simply reward you for all your years of hard work by being the person you groomed them to become.

Parenting an adult child might make you feel like you are wearing the parent tag only without exercising any of the rights or responsibilities. There are still so many opportunities to engage on a level that brings satisfaction and joy. As adults, your children may introduce you to things that will enhance your life. This is an opportunity to continue being their cheerleader while enriching your life.

Definitely, your children may decide to become parents someday. This is a great time to watch your children explore the exciting world of parenting. Whether you believe your child is ready to be a parent or how they decide to become a parent, this is a very exciting time in your family's life. George always says that grandchildren are our reward for not killing our children.

The arrival of grandchildren opens an exciting door that provides an opportunity to watch your children parent, but you also get a bird's eye view of watching their offspring grow and develop. While your grandchildren think the world of you, the same thing may not be said about your children's thoughts toward you. They love you, and you most certainly love them, but they are often confused by how loving and permissive you are with their offspring.

Let's face it, your parenting was not 100% fantastic, even though your children turned out 100% okay. There are a lot of things they are going to have to figure out on their own. That is because no two children are ever the same. Although children do not come with manuals, there are some parenting tips that we strongly suggest that you try. Time, place, and circumstances offer opportunities and limitations for how your children will parent their children. Your position as the parent of adult children is not to pass judgment on their decisions but to support their work as a parent.

Bearing this in mind, you must constantly remind yourself that you have had your opportunity to parent. It is now their turn to parent. Your children cannot and will not do it like you did because they are not you. Times and circumstances are different for your children, and they will need to make decisions about the rearing of their children. What was relevant and considered a priority in your days would differ when your children become parents. It does not make sense to follow through on practices that are irrelevant. You have their best interests at heart; this is something you are going to have to let them do on their own and in their own way.

Your behavior provides a positive example for your children to follow. In their younger years, the way you lived, the things you did set a precedent for who they want to be when they get older. And now that they are older, this has not changed. They are still learning from you even though they are now independent. You have a new status now as a grandparent. You have transitioned, and this is a point they may get to eventually. The goal of being a good model is not perfection but openness and honesty. It ensures that at whatever stage they are, they are living the best life possible.

Being honest with your thoughts and feelings is key to modeling healthy growth. There are going to be times when feelings of jealousy come up as the grands are spending time with the other grandparents or other family members. This is common as grandchildren have family members beyond you. And if you really love your grands, you will want them to know and have relationships with all their family members. The diversity they will experience with other family members will only strengthen them.

You must also ensure that you respect the feelings and opinions of your children regardless of your thoughts and ideas. This speaks to the fact that you recognize the value of your relationship with them and consider them equal despite the differences in years. You also recognize that your children are competent adults capable of setting goals for themselves and for their families.

Finally, remember to say those words that children need to hear. They may be older and running their own families, but they need to know that you still love them unconditionally, and they are killing it in the adulting department. They need to hear that you believe in them and their ability to be good parents. They need to know that you are proud of their achievements and that you believe they can still accomplish so much more. Positive words reinforce positive behavior. Your words are the best seeds to promote healthy growth.

Every moment in life is precious. This time in your life as a parent and possibly as a grandparent can be so rewarding because there are not many things you have to do in the parenting process. What started out as an idea grew to become a living breathing human who you loved with every fiber of your being and reared to the best of your ability. And when you think about things retrospectively, they grew up much too fast. Now you have time to watch them live out their lives.

Whether you see your grandchildren periodically through-out the year on special occasions or you live down the street from them, being in their lives is important. It is not the quantity of time that is spent on them, it is the quality of time. If you want to spend more time with them, make sure that you do as little as possible to burden their parents. This may mean traveling to where they live, opting to stay in a hotel instead of with your children, and visiting on times outside of holidays.

There are other opportunities to engage with your grandchildren without having to be in the same physical space. Regular phone calls can provide great opportunities to keep up with your grandchildren and to be relevant in their lives. Technology provides many opportunities to spend time with your grandchildren even if you do not live close to them. Special activities like reading them a bedtime story via video conferencing ensures that you are an integral part of their lives. Making these activities an integral part of your life is one way to reap the rewards of being a grandparent.

When you do get to spend time with your children and their children, stay in the moment. Have meaningful conversations that are sincere and considerate. Don't forget to share information about your life that your children and your grandchildren may not know. This will be a joy for them as they continue to grow and develop. Knowing about your family's background is beneficial to children's growth. Comfort and cherish each other. Embrace this family you have that has been bound together by blood, time and effort. This is one of life's sweetest gifts.

No child comes with a manual. Rearing a child is one of the most difficult but important tasks one will ever engage in. Each person is born with unique attributes. When children are born, many things determine how they act, their response to you and your instruction, and their approach to the world. All adults can help kids succeed in life provided they have a solid plan and are willing to carry it out.

"Children are on your knees for a moment,
and on your heart for a lifetime."

Emily Robinson

www.ingramcontent.com/pod-product-compliance
Lightning Source LLC
Chambersburg PA
CBHW020406130626
46549CB00006B/2456